Fort Washington in 1790
Reproduced from Charles Cist's "Cincinnati in 1851"

THE INDIAN CAPTIVITY
OF O. M. SPENCER

O. M. Spencer

Edited by
MILO MILTON QUAIFE

DOVER PUBLICATIONS, INC.
NEW YORK

Note to the Dover Edition

Dover Publications regrets the racist tinge of some comments in the Historical Introduction to the 1917 edition, which are included here unaltered for the sake of bibliographical completeness.

Published in Canada by General Publishing Company, Ltd., 30 Lesmill Road, Don Mills, Toronto, Ontario.

Published in the United Kingdom by Constable and Company, Ltd., 3 The Lanchesters, 162–164 Fulham Palace Road, London W6 9ER.

Bibliographical Note

This Dover edition, first published in 1995, is a slightly corrected republication of the work published in 1917 by The Lakeside Press (R. R. Donnelley & Sons Company), Chicago, which was itself a republication of the work first published serially in the *Western Christian Advocate*, Cincinnati, in 1834 (for further bibliographical details see the "Historical Introduction," below). The Publisher's Preface to the 1917 edition, concerning the series in which it was issued, has been omitted.

Library of Congress Cataloging-in-Publication Data

Spencer, Oliver M., 1781–1838.
The Indian captivity of O. M. Spencer / edited by Milo Milton Quaife.
    p.   cm.
". . . a slightly corrected republication of the work published in 1917 by the Lakeside Press (R.R. Donnelley & Sons Company), Chicago, which was itself a republication of the work first published serially in the Western Christian Advocate, Cincinnati, in 1834"—T.p. verso.
Includes index.
ISBN 0-486-28581-2
1. Spencer, Oliver M., 1781–1838—Captivity. 2. Indian captivities—Ohio River Valley. 3. Mohawk Indians—History. I. Quaife, Milo Milton, 1880–1959. II. Title.
E87.S746   1995
977.1'004975—dc20   94–34093
                                                CIP

Manufactured in the United States of America
Dover Publications, Inc., 31 East 2nd Street, Mineola, N.Y. 11501

Contents

Historical Introduction [1917]

A YEAR AGO in The Lakeside Classics was published the life narrative of the ambitious but unfortunate Sauk chieftain, Black Hawk, who dominated the last Indian war in the Old Northwest.[1] In attempting to evaluate the narrative the editor ascribed to it a two-fold historical significance. First, as a valuable source of information concerning the events with which it immediately deals; second, and of more importance, as presenting the viewpoint and state of mind of a typical representative of the red race upon the subject of its four-century conflict with the white man for the possession of the North American continent. The present volume deals with one aspect of the same struggle and, like its predecessor, possesses a two-fold significance. For the immediate events with which it deals it is a valuable source of historical information; it constitutes, moreover, a skillful presentation of a concrete instance of a class of events on the frontier which inspired the borderers with a deep and abiding loathing for their red neighbors.

When each of two races becomes imbued with the idea that it is suffering grievous wrongs at the hands of the other, as a consequence of which a deep-seated hatred and fear is conceived, the outcome, sooner or later, is certain—war to the knife to determine by an application of the law of might the question of right. Black Hawk's, *Autobiography* makes abundantly clear the red man's reason for hating his white rival. The present narrative, far less comprehensive than Black Hawk's, merely relates the story of the Indian captivity of a single white child. From this viewpoint alone it would not now, after the lapse of a century and a quarter, be worth reprinting. But the reader who is gifted with some knowledge of life and a fair endowment of imagination will see in it

---

[1][The 1916 edition of *Life of Black Hawk*, republished by Dover Publications, Inc., in 1994 (ISBN 0-486-28105-1).]

much more than the story of the fortunes of youthful Oliver Spencer. In it, as in a mirror, he will see the tremendous drama of the westward march of white America across the continent; the reduction of the wilderness from a home for wild beasts and savage men to the smiling abode of a peaceful civilization; the grim tenacity with which the untutored savage defended his native forest against the white flood slowly, but none the less surely, rolling on to engulf him; the play of human nature, the vicissitudes of human tragedy, the conflict of elemental forces;—all these things lie within the covers of the book for him who has the gift to perceive them.

To orient ourselves into the historical surroundings of Spencer's narrative we must make a brief survey of the concluding phase of the American Revolution. That famous struggle is commonly supposed to have ended with the year 1783. There was, however, a long aftermath, chiefly relating to the region west of the Alleghenies, so that in the West the Revolution may fairly be said to have ended with the conclusion of the Indian wars in 1795 and the transfer a year later of the British posts to American control.

The reasons for this prolongation of the Revolution in the West were numerous and complex. Since our present concern is only with a certain aspect of that struggle it will suffice to take note of the relations between the American people and the Indian tribes inhabiting the region north and west of the Ohio River. By the Treaty of Paris in 1783 the sovereignty of the United States to all the territory bounded by a line drawn through the middle of the Great Lakes and, on the west, the Mississippi River, was recognized. In the making of this treaty the tribes of American Indians had no voice. Yet during the Revolutionary War, Great Britain had actively instigated these tribes to join with her in waging war on the American settlers of western Pennsylvania and Virginia (the latter state then including modern West Virginia and Kentucky). The red man recognized no legal right on the part of Great Britain to cede their territory; on the contrary, her action in making peace with their joint enemy was regarded as a base desertion. As against civilized powers the new United States, by the treaty of 1783, acquired a perfect title to the territory lying east of the Mississippi and south of the Great Lakes; as against the red inhabitants of this vast region the American title had still to be established.

The task was immensely complicated by the presence of British sovereignty north of the Lakes and by certain relations between Great Britain and the new nation growing out of the treaty of 1783. There was naturally much irritation between the two newly separated branches of the English race. Neither nation sought to perform with entire fidelity the obligations it had assumed in the treaty of peace. Mutual recrimination over disregard of treaty rights led, before many years, to a condition which threatened a new war between England and America. Year after year the former declined to give up the northwestern posts, from which she had promised in 1783 to withdraw her armies "with all convenient speed." Her real reasons for this manifest infraction of treaty obligations were long withheld or dissembled. They are now recognized to have been due at first to a policy of opportunism; but at length to a natural desire to retain for Canada control of the fur trade of the interior; and as a means to this end to erect, from the vast region between the Ohio and the Lakes, a permanent Indian barrier state, which would forever stand as a buffer between the new American nation and Canada, and would insure to the latter domination over the tribes of the interior, and therewith the control of the Indian trade.

Thus, when the new American nation moved forward to the possession of its trans-Ohio territory it encountered the resistance not alone of the western tribes, but of these tribes backed by the moral, and to a certain extent the material, support of Great Britain. The government of the United States was weakened, too, by internal conditions. The Confederation was but a shadow, which grew steadily thinner until it completely dissolved about the year 1788. The transition to the new national government of the United States was effected in 1789, but it came into being burdened with debt, and justly fearful, in view of existing conditions, of speaking and acting boldly on behalf of the nation's interests.

The people, as contrasted with the government, manifested no such timidity in taking possession of their western inheritance. From the beginnings of colonization in Massachusetts and Virginia until the last step in the march across the continent, the zeal of the American people for westward expansion commonly outran that of the government. So, in the period under consideration, with the close of the Revolution the tide of white settlement, hitherto confined in the main to the south side of the Ohio, began to overflow its barrier. The expiring government of the Confederation responded to the desire of the people by providing, in the famous Ordinance of 1787, for civil government and for the ultimate organization of states in the Northwest Territory. In the same year, Congress sold to the Ohio Company five million acres of land, and in 1788 the company formally inaugurated its colonization enterprise by founding Marietta at the mouth of the Muskingum.

Therewith the American conquest of the Indian Northwest may be said fairly to have begun. The Revolution, a political success for the Americans, had entailed widespread economic disaster upon the colonists. Soldiers discharged from the armies, business men who had met with financial ruin, and in general all who found the conditions of life difficult in a time of general economic prostration, were eager for westward migration. Quickly on the heels of the Ohio Company of New Englanders and its settlement at the mouth of the Muskingum, came the formation of an association of New Jersey men for the exploitation of the tract of land between the two Miami rivers. In the spring of 1786, Benjamin Stites, formerly from New Jersey but then a resident of Redstone, Pennsylvania, engaged in a trading venture down the Ohio. At Limestone (now Maysville), Kentucky, he joined as volunteer a party of settlers in pursuit of a band of Indian marauders from across the Ohio. The pursuit, as commonly in such cases, failed of its immediate object, but it afforded Stites an opportunity to view the country between the Big and Little Miamis. By reason of the fact that it formed a part of the great highway taken by the rival war and raiding parties passing between the Kentucky settlements south of the Ohio and the Indian country north of that stream this region had come to be known as the "Miami slaughter house." Probably for this reason it had been carefully shunned by the numerous parties of settlers who had descended the Ohio in earlier years. Captivated by its charm and the evidences of its natural richness, Stites hastened to the East, bent on obtaining possession of "the slaughter house" region and there founding a colony.

In New York, Stites encountered a New Jersey congressman, John Cleves Symmes, who became actively interested in his project. A visit to the Ohio country, made the following year, convinced Symmes of the correctness of Stites' description of the tract in question. Under Symmes' leadership an association of twenty-five influential New Jersey men was formed to conduct the projected enterprise, and Congress was petitioned for an extensive grant of land. Without waiting for the action of Congress, Symmes proceeded to dispose of tracts of land to purchasers and prospective settlers, and in general to put the colonizing enterprise into execution. Because of his unbusiness-like procedure much confusion and trouble resulted, but into this we need not enter here. To Stites, Symmes conveyed ten thousand acres, to Mathias Denman a section of land opposite the mouth of Licking River, while for himself he reserved, as the site for a proposed metropolis, an extensive tract at the confluence of the Big Miami with the Ohio.

From these several projects three aspiring communities sprang at about the same time. Stites, first in the field, founded in November, 1788, the town of Columbia at the mouth of the Little Miami. A few weeks later Denman's project assumed visible form in the platting on his section of land of a town to which the Kentucky pedagogue, John Filson, gave the hybrid name Losantiville, signifying the town opposite the mouth of the Licking. A year or so later, Governor St. Clair quietly but firmly replaced the name Losantiville with the permanent title of Cincinnati. Slightly later than its rivals, Symmes' town was laid out at North Bend, now chiefly noted as the home and burial place of William Henry Harrison. Thus three towns, each expecting to become the future metropolis of the Ohio Valley, were started during the winter of 1789–90 in the "Miami slaughter house." Of the three, Cincinnati alone, midway both in point of geography and of chronology between its rivals, was destined to realize its founders' ambitious hopes. With the fortunes of North Bend we need not concern ourselves. Columbia, perhaps the most promising of all three, soon proved unable to hold its own with Cincinnati, its down-river neighbor. It lingered long as a village, until finally, in 1873, it was absorbed as a suburb by its erstwhile rival.

The most prominent settler of Columbia was Colonel Oliver Spencer, father of our narrator. Colonel Spencer was not only of the best English descent, but, a point of greater importance, he was entirely worthy of his ancestry. A native of Connecticut, he removed at an early age to Elizabethtown, New Jersey, where he married the daughter of Robert Ogden. The wife, like her husband, had excellent family connections, the Ogden family of New Jersey numbering a bishop, a chief justice, three judges, a general, and five colonels, besides numerous other worthies of lesser magnitude. Colonel Spencer engaged in the tannery business with his father-in-law and was rapidly acquiring wealth when the Revolution came to alter his whole future course of life. Of his military service the son speaks briefly. We need note in this connection only that while he served with credit throughout the war, rising to the rank of colonel in the continental service, he found himself at its close a ruined man, his capital dissipated, and his home and tannery (the latter one of the largest in America) gutted. Under such circumstances he turned a ready ear to the project for colonization on the Ohio, with the prospect it held out to men of energy of beginning life anew under more favorable circumstances than the settled East could offer. Cincinnatians still pride themselves on the high character of their forbears. To none can they point with more reason for pride than to the father of our narrator. Writing to Symmes on May 16, 1789, of Spencer's impending trip to view the Miami country, Jonathan Dayton dwelt upon the importance to their project of producing upon him a favorable impression, saying that there was not a person in New Jersey who could influence more settlers to follow him, and that many who were contemplating removal to the West were awaiting his report before deciding the momentous matter. The narrative of the son apprises us of the outcome of the journey. Colonel Spencer, like Stites before him, was charmed with the aspect of the country, and at once entered into arrangements for removing his family thither. Accordingly in October, 1790, the toilsome journey was begun, at first in wagons over the famous Pennsylvania Road, then by flatboat down the Youghiogheny and the Ohio to Columbia. The conditions of life in the new settlement, and in the neighboring Cincinnati in the year 1791 are sufficiently indicated by our narrative. In a word, the settlers' task of developing in the wilderness an abode of civilization was interrupted only by the ever present menace of Indian foray and massacre. With commendable promptness the new United States government took measures for the protection of the Miami settlements by establishing, in the summer of 1789, a post at Cincinnati. To it the name of Washington was given, and for a few years it constituted the chief military center of the United States. One might suppose that such an establishment in their midst would have rendered the settlers immune from Indian attack. For several years, however, life in the "Miami slaughter house" was sufficiently thrilling to satisfy even the most adventurous spirit, and many tales aside from those recorded by Spencer have come down to us of Indian attacks and slaughtering, not only at Columbia and North Bend, but in the very environs of Cincinnati itself. At the end of six months of life under such circumstances occurred the abduction of youthful Oliver Spencer, which, with the ensuing captivity, furnishes the principal theme of our narrative.

Before turning to the narrative itself, some notice may be taken of the manner in which the red men of the Northwest met the menace of the white advance, and precipitated both the first and the greatest Indian war in which the United States ever engaged. Although the record of our Indian wars constitutes on the whole a sorry story, we need not apologize for the justice of our cause in the first of the long series. If ever in history a war was unavoidable this one may fairly be so regarded. Ever since the close of the Revolution intermittent raiding and murdering had occurred. Early in 1790 the hovering war cloud burst in earnest, the natives forcing the issue by intercepting and plundering the boats conveying settlers down the Ohio. In July, Governor St. Clair called upon Kentucky, Pennsylvania, and Virginia for military assistance and set in motion his own forces. The main blow was directed from Fort Washington against Miamitown, on the site of the modern Fort Wayne. In October, General Harmar attacked the place with a force of some fourteen hundred men. The Indians drew back before the blow and their villages were destroyed. Harmar's main army was not engaged, but two considerable detachments from it waged bloody and unsuccessful conflicts with the red men. The army returned to Fort Washington, having lost in killed and wounded nearly three hundred men. At the best it had achieved a barren victory; at the worst a "mortifying failure." It was as though a blow had been dealt a nest of hornets. The Indians, momentarily stunned, were not cowed but only rendered the more furious.

Harmar had penetrated to the very center of Indian power. The natives promptly countered by massacring the settlers at Big Bottom near Marietta, on the night of January 2, 1791. Proffers of peace to the red men proving unavailing, the American government prepared for a second invasion of the Indian country to overawe the tribes and to establish in their midst, at the forks of the Maumee, a permanent fortress. In the autumn of 1791, General St. Clair set forth from Fort Washington on this mission, but instead of accomplishing it he led his army to the most terrible defeat in American military annals. The Indians were jubilant over the destruction of the American army. But, although they did not realize it, St. Clair's disaster had in no wise shaken the real military power of the United States; and the government, while still proffering the olive branch, set steadily about the task of organizing a new army which should succeed where those of Harmar and St. Clair had failed. Almost three years of preparation, under the vigorous leadership of General Wayne, ensued. At length, in the summer of 1794, his army set forth from Fort Washington to follow the track, but not to repeat the example, of its predecessors. On the site of the slaughter of St. Clair's army, Wayne built Fort Recovery; at the mouth of the Auglaize, where the weary months of Spencer's captivity were passed, the fortress grimly named Defiance was erected; at the Fallen Timbers on August 20, 1794, the power of the northwestern tribes was completely broken; at Miamitown, which Harmar had raided and St. Clair had vainly essayed to reach, another fort was built and the conqueror's name was permanently attached to the spot; finally, in council at Greenville in 1795, the tribesmen formally acknowledged Wayne as their conqueror and ceded to the United States the extensive tract covering, roughly speaking, the southern and eastern half of Ohio.

Thus peace was brought to the troubled frontier. To complete the work of Wayne's legion, in 1795 the Jay treaty with England was concluded, as the result of which Detroit and the other British frontier forts were surrendered to the United States in 1796. The American conquest of the Northwest, though far from completed, was now assured; and in general the political conditions which prevailed down to the outbreak of the War of 1812 were established.

To complete this summary view it remains to take some note of our author and his narrative. Of the author's later career I have learned but little. Investigation at Cincinnati would doubtless reveal much, but the opportunity for this has not been afforded me. The facts at hand, however, will sufficiently answer our purpose. Born in New Jersey about the year 1780, Spencer came west with his father, and Cincinnati became his permanent home. Readers of his narrative need not be informed that he became a preacher and that he learned to wield a facile pen. The *Cincinnati Directory* for 1819 lists him as president of two organizations, the American Bible Society and the Miami Exporting Company. Six years later the directory simply enters him as a Methodist Episcopal minister. He appears again in the directory for 1836; he died not long after this, for in 1838 he is referred to in the Draper Manuscripts of the Wisconsin Historical Library as "the late" O. M. Spencer.

Spencer's narrative was originally written for the *Western Christian Advocate* of Cincinnati. The publication of this paper began May 2, 1834. In its fourth issue Spencer's narrative was begun under the title *Indian Captivity. A true narrative of the Capture of the Rev. O. M. Spencer by the Indians, in the neighborhood of Cincinnati, written by himself, at the request of the editor.* By way of introduction, the editor stated that "brother Spencer" had been particularly requested to furnish the narrative, and to introduce it by an account of the westward migration of his father's family, noting the various difficulties and hardships of the pioneer life, that all might be enabled to profit "by a comparison of their numerous blessings with the privations, toils and dangers" of those who had gone before. The time and occasion of the narrative's appearance serve to make clear several things concerning its character and history. Written forty years after the occurrence of the events described, it does not have the value of a contemporary account; to offset this, however, the author was in the prime of life, his powers of observation and of expression were excellently trained, and the events of his captivity were of such a character as to make a deep impression upon his memory. Entire accuracy of detail on his part could scarcely be expected. Such errors as have been noted by the editor have been corrected in the footnotes of the present edition; the number of these is small, however, and the story bears evidence of being a truthful and for the most part accurate recital of fact. The indulgence in religious reflections which it displays may be explained partly on the ground of the author's calling; in part, probably, on that of the character of the audience for which it was written.

Once published, the story of Spencer's captivity seems to have enjoyed a remarkable popularity. As early as 1835 it was republished in a 32mo book of 157 pages by B. Waugh and T. Mason of New York, and the same year by G. W. Brice of Washington, Pennsylvania, as an octavo of 56 pages. Of the Waugh and Mason edition at least three reprints were issued, in London in 1836 and 1842 and in New York in 1854. About the year 1836 or 1838 another London reprint was brought out under a slightly altered title, accompanied by a theological introduction and scriptural illustrations of the original text, which was so changed as to be "scarcely recognizable." By 1854 a third edition of this reprint had appeared. The Wisconsin Historical Library possesses three copies of the work. One is the edition issued by G. W. Brice of Washington, Pennsylvania, in 1835; another was published in New York in 1842 by G. Love and P. P. Sanford for the Methodist Book Concern; the third copy, more modern in appearance but undated, was also published under the auspices of the Methodist Book Concern by Nelson and Phillips of New York and Hitchcock and Walden of Cincinnati. Though issued as different editions it is evident that the press work of these two latter volumes is identical. The introduction, common to both volumes and dated December 1, 1834, states that the narrative, originally written for the *Western Christian Advocate*, was copied into the *Christian Advocate and Journal* and was "at this time" in course of publication in several other papers. That other editions of the work were printed, of which no notice has come to the present editor, is not at all improbable.

For the present edition of the narrative I have ignored all of the editions in book form and have gone to the original source, the file of the *Western Christian Advocate* in the Wisconsin Historical Library. While no undue liberties have been taken in copying, the adoption of a typography and punctuation in accordance with modern usage has been deemed both proper and advisable. For these details, therefore, the editor is responsible, rather than the newspaper typesetters of 1834.

MILO M. QUAIFE.

Madison, Wisconsin.

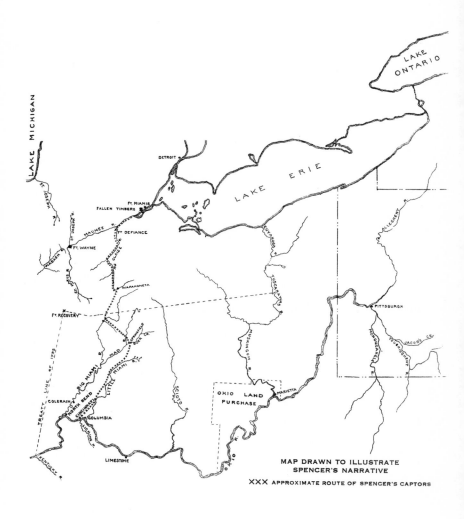

LAKE ONTARIO

LAKE MICHIGAN

LAKE ERIE

DETROIT

FT. MIAMIS
FALLEN TIMBERS
FT. DEFIANCE

MAUMEE
FT. WAYNE

ST. JOSEPH R.

WABASH R.

ST. MARY'S R.

WAPAKONETA

AUGLAIZE R.

FT. RECOVERY

ALLEGHENY

PITTSBURGH

CUYAHOGA

HOCKHOCKING

MUSKINGUM R.

MONONGAHELA

YOUGHIOGHENY R.

JACOB'S CR.

TREATY LINE OF 1795

BIG MIAMI

MAD R.

LITTLE MIAMI

MAD R.

COLERAIN
NORTH BEND
CINCINNATI
LICKING R.
COLUMBIA

SCIOTO

OHIO LAND PURCHASE

MARIETTA

LIMESTONE

KENTUCKY R.

OHIO

MAP DRAWN TO ILLUSTRATE
SPENCER'S NARRATIVE

XXX APPROXIMATE ROUTE OF SPENCER'S CAPTORS

The Indian Captivity of O. M. Spencer

CHAPTER I

It was on a pleasant day in October of the year 1790, when only nine years of age, I mounted the leading horse attached to the foremost of two wagons destined for the "far West," in which my mother and sisters were seated; and in which were stowed such articles of household furniture as were indispensable to the comfort of a family, and which could not then be easily procured west of the Allegheny. With spirits naturally buoyant, pleased with the novelty of traveling, from which I anticipated a great deal of pleasure, the few tears which I shed on quitting forever the home of my childhood were soon dried up; and I wondered not a little at the sober sadness of my father, the deep sighs of my mother, and the frequent sobs of my sisters, whose feelings and expectations I supposed would naturally correspond with mine.

My father had descended from one of the first families who left England on account of the persecutions for religious opinions, in the reign of the second Charles, to seek in the unbroken wilds of New England an asylum from oppression, and to rear a temple to the God of their fathers in which they might worship Him according to the dictates of their own consciences.

Inheriting the spirit of his ancestors, he was among the first to resist the pretensions of Great Britain, and to arm in defense of our rights and liberties. Having signalized himself on several occasions, particularly in the battle of Springfield, New Jersey, at the head of a battalion of militia, he was appointed by Congress to the command of a regiment, which he led in the battles of Brandywine, Germantown, and Monmouth; and at the head of which he continued until the close of the war.

Before entering the continental army he possessed a small fortune, the fruits of his industry in a lucrative business; but of this a large amount was destroyed by the enemy, and more than ten thousand

1

dollars, advanced by him in specie to pay and clothe his regiment, were repaid to him by Congress in continental money, on which he sustained a total loss. Like many of his companions in arms, after encountering the dangers and enduring the hardships of a protracted war, Colonel Spencer found himself at its close reduced from affluence to comparative poverty; but with them, too, he enjoyed the proud satisfaction of having aided in achieving that independence which laid the foundation of our national greatness and prosperity, and the hope of perpetuating to his children's children the blessings of civil and religious liberty.

With impaired health and injured constitution he again engaged in business, hoping in time to retrieve his losses, and trusting in the honor and the justice of the government to pay his equitable claims against it; but in this hope and in this confidence he was deeply disappointed. After toiling many years with little success, hearing the flattering accounts then in circulation of the beauty and fertility of the Miami country, he determined to explore it. He did visit it in 1789, and being much pleased with it determined on making it his future residence. Previously to his leaving home he had disposed of his certificates for his military services at one-third part of their nominal value, and vested their proceeds in Miami lands; and now, having purchased some lots and erected a cabin in Columbia for the reception of his family, he returned home to effect their removal.

Neither my father's description of the Miami country, nor the most glowing representations almost daily published of "the land flowing with milk and honey," could have prevailed with my mother to abandon the home of her fathers, "her own, her native land"; the early companions of her youth; her faithful and long-tried friends; and, above all, some of her own daughters, who had married and settled around her: but she was a most exemplary wife, sensible and intelligent, possessing great resolution and uncommon fortitude, and withal, a woman of deep piety; and being satisfied that the step on which my father had decided was necessary, she acquiesced in that decision without murmuring.

The first few days of our journey passed very heavily. There was, indeed, much that amused and even delighted me, but we had little conversation; my thoughtless whistle and the quaint expressions and occasional humorous sayings of the driver, an old soldier, being all that for hours broke upon the stillness of the lonely woods, or varied the dull monotony of our rumbling wheels. Gradually, however, the family became more cheerful. Dwelling less upon the past, their thoughts began to be occupied with their present condition and future prospects, and they now found much to interest them and to render their journey agreeable.

From Mendham, a small village in East Jersey (our late residence) our route lay through Easton and Harrisburg. [1] Passing these towns, we soon reached the formidable mountains which separate the waters of the Atlantic states from those of the Mississippi Valley; and here we were called to exert all our fortitude, and to exercise all our patience. Those who now travel from Philadelphia to Pittsburgh, ascending easily and gliding rapidly over the Allegheny, along the broad and finely-paved road, finding at convenient distances commodious inns and excellent entertainment, can form but a faint idea of the difficulties and dangers encountered, and the fatigue and privations which more than forty years since were endured by emigrants to the West, from extremely bad roads and worse accommodations. Often since, when traveling the road from Chambersburg to Pittsburgh, in a comfortable stage, at a rapid rate, over the precipitous Laurel Hill and formidable Allegheny, I have been forcibly struck with the contrast; and as I occasionally caught a glimpse of the ancient narrow road winding among the trees, now rising, now descending abruptly by steep steps of solid rock, I thought it scarcely possible that any vehicle had ever passed over it. It was traveled, certainly, at the risk of limbs and even of life.

It was after a day's fatiguing journey over the worst portion of this road, in which we were delayed more than an hour in repairing damages to one of our wagons from a disastrous overset, that night overtook us in the midst of a dense forest more than two miles from any habitation. This to our family, who had never known the want of a comfortable shelter, was a novel and an almost appalling circumstance. To increase their apprehension the wolves commenced a most hideous howling, and their fruitful imaginations soon added a host of bears and panthers and robbers. Soon, however, with the aid of a tinder box we kindled a large fire; and after a slender repast of biscuit and cheese, with a little pure water from an adjoining brook, we retired to our wagons and in deep sleep soon forgot our cares and apprehension.

We had slept perhaps two hours when, awakening about eleven o'clock, I discovered that my bed-fellow, a nephew a year my elder, had

---

[1] The Spencer family followed the great highway to the West first laid out by General Forbes' army in the campaign against Fort Duquesne (modern Pittsburgh) in 1758. Later known as the Pennsylvania Road, this was one of the two chief highways from the seaboard to the Ohio, the other being the famous Cumberland Road. For a detailed and interesting history of the Pennsylvania Road, see Archer B. Hulbert, *The Old Glade (Forbes's) Road* (Cleveland, 1903).

left the wagon. After waiting some time, as he did not return I called him, and repeating my calls louder and still louder soon awoke the family. Search was made for him in every probable direction, but in vain; loud calls and the firing of guns received no response save the louder howling of the wolves, whom we now confidently believed had torn him to pieces. But in the midst of our alarm and distress we received the welcome information of his safety. He had walked in his sleep, with bare feet and almost naked, in a cold night of October, to a house about two miles in advance of us on our road, had knocked at the door and was admitted, but did not awake until the screams of its inmates, some of whom were terror-stricken, aroused him. Recovering himself, he soon convinced them that he was not an apparition, but a real "spirit of health," and as it was now late, was kindly accommodated with a bed for the night.

It is a fact within the recollection of many of us, that not more than twenty-five years since, before the application of steam to the propulsion of vessels, almost the only conveyance on the western waters was by keel and flat boats. The latter, being cheap and easily built and intended wholly for conveyance down the Ohio and Mississippi, were always sought by families descending these rivers.[2] And as there were several places along the Monongahela at which these boats were built, and where they could be obtained on better terms than at Pittsburgh, instead of taking the direct road to that place we took a southwesterly direction to Jacob's Creek, a branch of the Youghiogheny. Here, having arrived and waited more than a month for the building of a boat, and for a rise of water, we embarked for Columbia; and in company with another family, and numbering together about sixteen souls, soon found ourselves quietly gliding down the beautiful waters of the Ohio.

To the early immigrant it must be truly pleasing to mark the great and rapid changes which within his remembrance have been wrought, not only along the rivers, but in the whole valley of the Mississippi. To contrast the once unbroken wilderness, in its solitude undisturbed save by the howl of the wolf, the terrific scream of the panther, or the appalling yell of the savage, with the cultivated fields and comfortable farmhouses, the neat villages, the populous towns, and even large cities which he now beholds, risen as by magic and swarming with inhabitants, active, industrious, and enterprising; to hear the "busy hum," and note the constant bustle of commerce; and where the sluggish flat or

---

[2]For a good account of the river traffic of the Ohio in the pioneer period, concerning which Spencer speaks briefly here, see Archer B. Hulbert, *Waterways of Westward Expansion: The Ohio River and Its Tributaries* (Cleveland, 1903).

laboring keel seemed scarcely to advance, to see the stately steamer proudly stemming the rapid current, or urged down it at so swift a speed as seemingly to bring near places the most remote, and to overcome, in the short time of eight days, a distance to perform which once required three months, even in the best keelboat, with all the aid of sails and oars and warps.

Yet there are times when he enjoys a melancholy pleasure in his recollections of the past; when the varied scenery of the West was beheld by him in all its loveliness, and in all its primeval grandeur. When, unused to the destructive wave of the steamer or the more desolating axe of the later settler, the unbroken banks of the beautiful Ohio were seen, on one side, first gently sloping from the pebbled shore fringed with willows, then gradually ascending a few rods, covered with cottonwood, linden, and soft maple, then with steep ascent rising to their summit, crowned with elm and sycamore, and bounding the ample bottom, where the stately beech and poplar, the noble ash and walnut, the tall hickory, and the majestic oak had withstood the storms of ages. Here too were seen the flowering buckeye, the guarded honey-tree dropping its sweets, the fragrant spicewood, the sassafras affording tea and the maple yielding sugar to the early settlers. On the other side were seen the hills bounding these fertile bottoms and forming a vast amphitheater; sometimes breaking abruptly in huge masses of rock, interspersed with cedar and opposing an unyielding barrier to the stream; and now terminating with precipitous descent, covered with lofty trees quite down to the water's edge. There seemed to be blended with the beauty and the lovely scenery of the Ohio, inspiring pleasure, a wildness and a solitude which struck the beholder with mingled fear and awe.

Such were our sensations as we descended the Ohio. Indeed, there was with us a prevailing sense of loneliness; a feeling of apprehension, which after we left Pittsburgh was interrupted only as we passed by Wheeling, Marietta, Kanawha, Gallipolis, Limestone (now Maysville), and a few other intermediate settlements, to our place of destination. But although we were sometimes alarmed, and often apprehended an attack from the Indians, we saw none, nor but few signs of any, during our passage; and providentially meeting with no disaster, arrived safely at Columbia early in December, 1790.

CHAPTER II

It is, perhaps, unknown to many that the broad and extensive plain stretching along the Ohio from the Crawfish to the mouth, and for three miles up the Little Miami, and now divided into farms, highly cultivated, was the ancient site of Columbia, a town laid out by Major Benjamin Stites, its original proprietor; and by him and others once expected to become a large city, the great capital of the West. From Crawfish, the small creek forming its northwestern boundary, more than one mile up the Ohio, and extending back about three-fourths of a mile, and half way up the high hill which formed a part of its eastern and northern limits, the ground was laid off into blocks containing each eight lots of half an acre, bounded by streets intersecting at right angles. The residue of the plain was divided into lots of four and five acres for the accommodation of the town. Over this plain, on our arrival, we found scattered about fifty cabins, flanked by a small stockade nearly half a mile below the mouth of the Miami, together with a few block-houses for the protection of the inhabitants, at suitable distances along the bank of the Ohio.

Whoever has traveled the turnpike leading from Cincinnati to Milford, after crossing the large culvert over Crawfish and passing the cluster of buildings beyond it, has seen, a few hundred yards farther on, near the foot of the hill on the left of that road, an old hewed log house, with four small windows in front, until within a few years past shaded with large willows. About six feet north of that house, built forty-two years since and long the residence of my father, stood the small log

6

cabin, our first humble shelter on our landing. Its narrow doors of thick oak plank, turning on stout wooden hinges and secured with strong bars braced with timber from the floor, formed a safe barrier to the entrance below; while above, on every side, were portholes or small embrasures from which we might see and fire upon the enemy. Of windows we had but two, containing only four panes of glass each, in openings so small that any attempt to enter them by force must have proved fatal to an assailant.

We had occupied our new habitation about a month, adding greatly to its accommodation and supplying many conveniences around us; indeed, we began to submit to the inconveniences, privations, hardships, and dangers common to the pioneers of the West without much repining; and having heard of no disturbances by Indians in our immediate neighborhood for some time previously, felt little apprehension of danger. But our fears were suddenly aroused by the news of an attack made by several hundred Indians on Dunlap's Station (now Colerain), fifteen or twenty miles northwest of Cincinnati, then garrisoned by a few inhabitants and thirty or forty soldiers under the command of Lieutenant Kingsbury.[3] This intelligence was brought by Mr. John S. Wallace (now Colonel Wallace, our respected fellow citizen), who, at the risk of his life, left the garrison at night, passed unperceived through the enemy, and safely reached Cincinnati the same night. Of the volunteers, who marched immediately to relieve the garrison, one company was from Columbia. All were well mounted and armed with rifles, knives, and some even with tomahawks, and dressed in hunting shirts, moved off in single file. Arriving at Colerain too late to encounter the enemy, who a few hours before had raised the siege, they after a short pursuit returned home, and by no means allayed our apprehensions by their fearful accounts of Indian warfare and savage barbarity.

We had often heard of the cruelties practiced by the Indians; but the details of the burning of Mr. Abner Hunt, whom they had taken prisoner a few hours before their attack on the garrison, shocked us beyond measure. It is much easier to conceive than to describe the feelings of the garrison when, after being urged and entreated by the wretched man to purchase their own safety and above all his life by surrendering to the enemy, they saw him led off and witnessed the

---

[3]Jacob Kingsbury, later colonel and commander of the military forces of the United States in the Northwest. With the exception of the four years 1783–87 Kingsbury's military service was continuous from 1775 until 1815. Many of his private papers are preserved in the Library of Congress and in that of the Chicago Historical Society.

fearful preparations for torture; or the heart-sickening anguish of hope suddenly extinguished, the mute despair of the prisoner as he heard the decided, though reluctant, refusal of the garrison to save his life at the certain loss of their own. The Indians had tied their prisoner to a sapling within sight of the garrison, who distinctly heard his screams, and built a large fire so near as to scorch him, inflicting the most acute pain; then as his flesh from the action of the fire and the frequent application of live coals became less sensible, making deep incisions in his limbs, as if to renew his susceptibility of pain; answering his cries for water to allay the extreme thirst caused by burning, by fresh tortures; and finally, when exhausted and fainting, death seemed approaching to release the wretched prisoner, terminating his sufferings by applying flaming brands to his naked bowels. In this siege, which lasted two days, the Indians suffered severely in killed and wounded, without inflicting any serious personal injury on the garrison, whose principal loss was in cattle, destroyed or driven off by the enemy. The attack on Dunlap's Station was followed by successive depredations and murders by the Indians.

In the ensuing spring they attacked several boats, killed many persons, and took some prisoners on the Ohio. Individuals were killed or made prisoners even on the outlots of Cincinnati and near the mouth of Deer Creek, and many were the "hair-breadth escapes" from captivity or death. It is few years since, that near the turnpike three miles above this city might be seen the large elm behind which some Indians stood concealed, and as he passed on horseback, seized and made —— Bailey prisoner: and not more than five miles beyond, where the same road crosses the narrows of Little Miami, only a few months since I recognized the spot where the brave but unfortunate Newell fell a victim to the rifle and scalping knife of the savage.

The successful expedition of General Scott of Kentucky against the Indians on the Wabash in May, 1791, had but little effect on the tribes north of us, whose boldness and daring remained unchecked.[4] Early in the summer of that year they stole our horses, two in number, from a shed adjoining our cabin; and only a few days afterwards we narrowly escaped the total massacre of our family. We had just ended our evening's

---

[4]In May, 1791, General Charles Scott of Kentucky, accompanied by Colonel James Wilkinson, led 800 mounted Kentuckians in a raid upon the Wea villages on the Wabash of which Ouiatanon was the leading center. The raid was entirely successful in accomplishing its immediate object, the destruction of the Wea towns, but as Spencer points out it did not serve to check in any way the hostility displayed by the northwestern tribes in general toward the Americans.

repast and were about to rise from our table when one of my sisters, hearing as she believed the almost noiseless tread of approaching footsteps, casting her eyes upon the door and perceiving as she thought the latch gently rising, sprang up and, seizing it, held it down until the doors were barred. Immediate preparations were made for defense. Our lights were instantly extinguished, and while the females of our family sought safety by covering themselves with beds the men, three in number, with a rifle and two muskets manned the portholes above; and by frequently moving to the different sides of the house endeavored to impress the Indians with an idea of our strength. The tread of the Indians was now distinctly heard, and the forms of two or three of them were indistinctly seen gliding through the darkness. Their intention, no doubt, had been to take us by surprise; and, opening the back door silently, to have first fired upon us, and then to have rushed into the house and with their tomahawks have completed the work of destruction; but failing in this, being too few to take us by assault, seeing no opportunity of injuring us, and probably, too, not wishing to alarm the town without first effecting some mischief, they soon stole off and disappeared. But a few minutes, however, had elapsed before we heard the crack of rifles within two hundred yards of us, followed by the shrill war-whoop of the Indians. Three musket shots in quick succession soon sounded an alarm and in ten minutes about thirty men had assembled at the cabin of Ensign Bowman on the hill side, a short distance west of us. They found the family in great consternation. The Indians had fired into the house through an opening between the logs, and guided by the light within, had wounded Mrs. Bowman slightly in her body.

At sunrise of the following day a small party pursued the Indians, whose number from their trails did not exceed six; and toward noon, finding their tracks quite fresh and judging that they now were almost in view of the enemy, moved cautiously, half bent and straining their eyes as if they would look through every tree before them. Suddenly at the sharp crack of one of their own rifles, as by one impulse each sprang behind a tree, waiting a few moments in breathless suspense the appearance of the Indians. At this moment a huge bear was seen bounding off a few rods from their left, and the disappointed marksman was heard muttering curses on his rifle for deceiving his expectations. The rest of the party, however, who had strong doubts of his courage and believed that he had availed himself of this opportunity to avoid an encounter with the enemy, were deeply incensed, and could with difficulty be prevented from anticipating the decision of a court martial by inflicting summary punishment on the culprit who in one unlucky moment, as they confidently believed, had deprived them of the certain spoils of victory.[5]

Soon after the failure of Colonel Harmar's expedition the government had determined to send a powerful force against the Indians, sufficient at once to reduce them to subjection. Troops were daily arriving at Cincinnati so that in September, 1791, a large force, consisting of regulars, levies, and militia, under the command of General St. Clair, then governor of the Northwestern Territory, was ready to march against the enemy. From the known experience and distinguished reputation of the general as a soldier, and the character of the officers under his command, the greater part of whom had seen service, complete success was confidently anticipated; and in the full expectation that the Indians would be humbled into submission, and apprehending no danger while a force so formidable guarded their frontiers, the inhabitants of the Miami Valley enjoyed for some weeks tranquillity and repose.

From Cincinnati, the march of General St. Clair's army was in a direction a little west of north. Passing Fort Hamilton, which they had previously built on the site of the present town of Hamilton, and crossing the Great Miami at that place, they advanced about twenty-six miles, and having built Fort St. Clair near the present town of Eaton, marched twenty-two miles farther north and erected Fort Jefferson.

Their progress unavoidably had been slow, not only from the delay of building forts but from the nature of the ground over which they passed, where much labor was required in opening and making a road for the passage of their artillery and baggage wagons. They had suffered some detention, too, from the want of supplies; sometimes failing from the neglect of contractors and at others interrupted or cut off by the enemy. Pursuing the direct course to the Indian villages on the Maumee River, or Miami of Lake Erie, they had on the third of November advanced about thirty miles northwestwardly of Fort Jefferson and within forty-five miles of the nearest town of the enemy; while the inhabitants of the Miami settlements, who had almost daily heard of the progress of the army and who confidently anticipated their complete success, were anxiously expecting soon to hear that they had achieved a glorious and decisive victory. But inexpressible was their disappointment and deep was their consternation when on the evening of the sixth of November

---

[5]A somewhat different contemporary story of the result of the pursuit of the Indians is preserved in the Draper Mss. of the Wisconsin Historical Library. It relates that two of the pursuers came upon two Indians engaged in cooking venison a few miles from Cincinnati. Both white men fired at the same instant upon their quarry. Unhappily, however, both had picked the same man, and while he fell dead, pierced by both balls, his companion darted into the adjoining thicket and escaped. The whites returned to Columbia bearing as a trophy the first scalp which was brought to the infant settlement.

accounts reached them of the total defeat of the army; accounts confirmed every hour by some of its fugitives, with more fearful details of Indian barbarity, and followed almost immediately by the broken remains of the army, who, marching night and day, reached Cincinnati on the eighth.

The battle of the fourth of November, 1791, and the disastrous defeat of General St. Clair's army, form a part of the early history of the West; most of their details have been told, and need not here be repeated. I may, however, be allowed to state some facts not generally known, related by officers who were in that engagement; and others communicated to me afterward, while a captive among the Indians, by prisoners taken in that battle.

On the afternoon of the third of November the main body of the army, principally regulars and levies, encamped on the south side of a branch of the Wabash in two lines, distant from each other seventy or eighty yards, fronting the stream and extending along it, and within a few hundred feet of it, about three hundred and fifty yards. On the north side of the stream and a quarter of a mile in advance of the main army the militia under Colonel Oldham were posted; and beyond them at a suitable distance an advance guard of a company of regulars, under Captain Slough, was placed. Some time before light of the ensuing day the approach of the Indians in considerable numbers compelled this guard to fall back upon the militia. But although this fact was reported to General Butler, and although he was advised that an attack would certainly be made upon the army that morning, he seemed to have either regarded the information "as an idle tale," or to have relied so confidently in the strength of the army as to have considered it invincible.[6]

The morning of the fourth had dawned; the shrill fife and rolling drum had sounded the cheerful reveille; the troops, as was their daily practice, had manned their lines and stood under arms in battle array until after the sun had risen, when, no enemy appearing, they had retired, some to prepare their breakfasts or perform various other duties, and not a few to lounge in their tents. Suddenly the sharp crack of a thousand rifles, mingled with the hideous and deafening yells of the

---

[6]The incident touched upon constitutes one of the deplorable affairs in the history of the United States army. Butler, second in command of St. Clair's army, had taken bitter offense at his chief. Apparently he chose to conceal from St. Clair the news brought to him by Captain Slough of the advance of the Indian army, desiring the disgrace of his chief even though at the risk of the destruction of the American army. As a consequence the army had been destroyed five days before St. Clair received Captain Slough's report of the Indian advance upon it. The most charitable explanation which can be offered concerning General Butler's course is the suggestion that sanity had deserted him. On the whole affair, see Hulbert, *op. cit.* 148–52.

Indians, announced but too certainly that the militia in front were attacked in great force by the enemy. The drums of the encampment instantly beat to arms and the soldiers hastened to their posts; but scarcely had the troops formed and prepared for action when the routed militia, closely pursued by the savages, rushed through the front line into the camp, throwing that line into a confusion from which it could not be entirely recovered. Following up their advantage the Indians boldly advanced upon the front as if determined to force it, but meeting with a firm resistance and receiving several well-directed volleys from our men, were compelled to fall back. Our troops now for a short time fought bravely, but contending under great disadvantages against superior numbers, soon became disheartened. Occupying an elevated piece of ground, while they stood openly exposed to the destructive fire of the Indians from behind trees and logs their own principally passed entirely over the enemy; their bullets, and particularly the balls of their cannon, being afterwards found lodged in the bodies and limbs of the trees thirty feet above the ground. Early in the action the troops were entirely surrounded by the Indians, who, while some of them retreated from one side of the camp before the charge of the bayonet, others rushed in on the opposite side or on the flanks, killing and scalping the wounded. These charges were repeated several times, but always with great loss to our troops; indeed, it seemed as if the Indians fled at first before their charge as if to draw them out some distance from their lines, then suddenly turning upon them, compel them to retreat, leaving their wounded to certain destruction.

It was during one of these charges that the brave but unfortunate General Butler was killed. He had been mortally wounded early in the battle and carried to his tent; and determining to sell his life as dearly as possible, was there placed in a reclining posture, with a pair of pistols by his side. In pursuing our troops, retreating in their turn, two warriors at once espied him, and both anxious to plunder his person as well as to take his scalp, rushed forward, the one only a few feet in advance of the other. The foremost Indian had but just entered his tent when the general, leveling one pistol, shot him dead; but while in the act of presenting the second, received the stroke of the hurled tomahawk of the other and instantly expired. A few rods from this tent Captain Ford, the only surviving officer of artillery, severely wounded and disabled, was providentially saved from a similar fate by having been placed against a large tree on the opposite side from that on which the Indians were then charging.

The fatal rifles of the enemy were still dealing death, and their tomahawks and scalping knives, completing the work of destruction, had killed nearly half of the soldiers and more than three-fourths of the officers when General St. Clair, satisfied that further resistance would be hopeless, determined on a retreat as the only means of saving the remnant of the army. The remaining troops were now formed under Colonel Darke, and vigorously charging the Indians, who gave way on their right and left, gained the road and commenced a retreat, which soon increased to a flight. Not only were the artillery and baggage abandoned, but even the wounded, with very few exceptions, were left to their fate. Each, struggling for his own preservation, thought not of the safety of others. The life of Captain Ford, however, was saved by the devoted attachment of one of his men, who, placing him upon a horse, bore him safely from the battle-ground; while Dr. Richard Allison, senior surgeon of the army, than whom none were more brave, humane, and benevolent, mounted on his own powerful and spirited horse with his waiter seated behind him, brought off from the field Captain Shaylor and three others, who, laying hold of the mane and tail of the noble animal, were enabled to escape the pursuit of the enemy.

Of about 1500 men who engaged in battle on that fatal morning, 630, including 37 officers, were killed; and 244, including 30 officers, were wounded. Besides these, a number of pack-horsemen, wagoners, and others attached to the army were killed; and of nearly 200 women, principally its followers, 3 only escaped, about 50 were killed, and the residue were made prisoners.[7] Had the Indians pursued their advantage they might easily have cut off the whole remnant of the troops, many of whom, soon after the retreat commenced, threw away their arms, betaking themselves to flight. But having signally defeated the army and satiated for a time their thirst for carnage, the greater part of them remained to plunder the camp; while those who pursued the flying troops, cutting off the stragglers and scalping the wounded, after following them about four miles, fearing they should not obtain their share of the spoil, suddenly gave over the pursuit and returned to the encampment.

Here, after plundering and stripping the dead, securing everything that they could individually appropriate to themselves, and after being gorged with feasting, principally on slaughtered bullocks, they began to drink and carouse; and while some became stupid, others, growing

---

[7]Probably no other statement could cast a clearer light upon the mismanagement which terminated in the ruin of St. Clair's army than this one concerning the presence of these women.

more ferocious as they felt the influence of the "fire water," rent the air with their hideous war-whoops, acted over their savage feats, cutting and mangling the dead bodies; and finding many not yet dead from their wounds, tore out the hearts of some and throwing others into the fire terminated their sufferings. A few Indians, less ferocious, dressing themselves in the uniforms of the dead officers, strutted about the encampment. One of these I afterward saw while a prisoner among the Shawnees, wearing the dress coat of a field officer of infantry, with silver epaulets on his shoulders and a watch suspended from each ear. With one hand taking hold of the facing of his coat, he said to me, "Me kill um"; and with the other smiting his breast, vociferated, "Captain Walker! Great man me!" The Indians were led by several brave and experienced chiefs; and besides the infamous renegade, Girty,[8] and the notorious Colonel Elliott,[9] I was told that Captain McKee[10] of the royal American and several of the British officers were in the battle.

The defeat of General St. Clair was not followed by those disastrous consequences which at first were apprehended. Strong garrisons being kept up at Hamilton, St. Clair, and even Fort Jefferson, afforded to the inhabitants of the Miami settlements great protection; while in Fort Washington several companies of troops more than were necessary for its defense not only gave constant security to the citizens of Cincinnati, but the means of repelling any inroads of the enemy, and of extending aid in case of attack to other villages. Perhaps, too, a considerable loss which the Indians suffered a few weeks after their victory may have operated as a check to their inroads upon the frontiers. This was effected by General Scott, who with a body of mounted men, principally Kentucky volunteers, proceeded to the battleground and taking by surprise

---

[8]Apparently Simon Girty, eldest of three brothers—Simon, James, and George—who, for a generation were objects of fear and loathing to the American frontiersmen. They were natives of Pennsylvania who were captured by an Indian raiding party in 1756, and who during the Revolution upheld the British cause. For an account of the brothers' careers, see Consul W. Butterfield, *History of the Girtys* (Cincinnati, 1890).

[9]Matthew Elliott was a native of Ireland who removed at an early age to Pennsylvania. He became an Indian trader, and early in the Revolution was carried prisoner to Detroit by a band of Wyandot. He thereupon allied himself with the British cause and later claimed he had gone voluntarily to Detroit. At first the British doubted his fidelity but he lived down this suspicion and became one of the most noted British agents on the frontier. How the Kentuckians regarded him was shown in 1814, when, on the capture of Amherstburg after Perry's victory on Lake Erie, they completely wrecked his house and furniture.

[10]Alexander McKee was, like the Girtys, a native of Pennsylvania who sided with the British during the Revolution. He became an agent in the British Indian Department and acquired much influence over the western tribesmen, which he employed, after the Revolution, to incite them against the Americans. He had a large trading house on the Maumee, where he received Indian refugees from Wayne's victory of Fallen Timbers in 1794.

about one-fourth of the enemy's late force (admitted by them to be two thousand) whom he there found still carousing, signally defeated them, killing more than two hundred and recovering, besides, six or seven hundred muskets found in the camp and along the road, some baggage, tents, and a part of the artillery; several pieces of which were thrown by the Indians into the Wabash, where, I believe, they were afterwards found.

CHAPTER III

FEW ONLY OF those who now behold Cincinnati, in point of extent, population, and the number, beauty, and permanency of its buildings the seventh city in the United States, have any correct idea of what it was more than forty-three years since. About the twenty-second of February, 1791, when I first saw it, it contained not more than forty dwellings, all log cabins, and not exceeding two hundred and fifty inhabitants. In the southeastern part of the town, near the site of his present dwelling, stood the cabin of Mr. D. E. Wade in the midst of the forest trees; and just below on the first bank, between the mouth of Deer Creek and Lawrence Street, were scattered among the trees four or five more cabins. Between Eastern Row (a narrow street enlarged into Broadway) and Main Street on Front and Columbia streets there were about twenty log houses; and on Sycamore and Main, principally on the second bank or hill, as it was called, there were scattered about fifteen cabins more. At the foot of this bank, extending across Broadway and Main streets, were large ponds, on which as lately as the winter of 1798 I have seen boys skating. All the ground from the foot of the second bank to the river between Lawrence Street and Broadway, and appropriated to the fort, was an open space on which, although no trees were left standing, most of their large trunks were still lying. On the top, and about eighty feet distant from the brow of the second bank, facing the river, stood Fort Washington, occupying nearly all the ground between Third and Fourth streets and between Ludlow Street and Broadway.

This fort, of nearly a square form, was simply a wooden fortification, whose four sides or walls, each about one hundred and eighty feet long, were constructed of hewed logs erected into barracks two stories high, connected at the corners by high pickets, with bastions or blockhouses also of hewed logs, and projecting about ten feet in front of each side of the fort, so that the cannon placed within them could be brought to rake its walls. Through the center of the south side or front of the fort was the principal gateway, a passage through this line of barracks about twelve feet wide and ten feet high, secured by strong wooden doors of the same dimensions. Appended to the fort on its north side, and enclosed with high palisades extending from its northeast and northwest corners to a blockhouse, was a small triangular space in which were constructed shops for the accommodations of the artificers. Extending along the whole front of the fort was a fine esplanade about eighty feet wide and enclosed with a handsome paling on the brow of the bank, the descent from which to the lower bottom was sloping, about thirty feet. The front and sides of the fort were whitewashed and at a small distance presented a handsome and imposing appearance. On the eastern side were the officers' gardens, finely cultivated, ornamented with beautiful summer houses, and yielding in their season an abundance of vegetables.

The twenty-second of February, 1792, was celebrated by the officers at Fort Washington, with their ladies and those of Columbia and Cincinnati, altogether about twelve, by what was then in the West considered a splendid ball, preceded by the firing of cannon, the discharge of rockets, and the exhibition of a variety of fireworks; and in riding, visiting, dancing, and other amusements they soon forgot their wounds and the dangers of their late disastrous campaign.

Often as I sit securely in the house of God, the spacious temple of the Most High, surveying the hundreds that surround me fearlessly raising their notes of praise and tranquilly worshiping the Father of Mercies, the days of other years and scenes long, long past recur to my mind with all the vividness of recent occurrence. Then fresh in my remembrance is the rude log house, the first humble sanctuary of the first settlers of Columbia, standing amidst the tall forest trees on the beautiful knoll where now may be seen a graveyard and the ruins of a Baptist meeting house of later years. There on the holy sabbath, we were wont to assemble to hear the word of life; but our fathers met with their muskets and rifles, prepared for action and ready to repel any attack of the enemy. And while the watchman on the walls of Zion was uttering his faithful and pathetic warning, the sentinels without, at a few rods' distance, with measured step were now pacing their walks, and now standing with strained eyes endeavoring to pierce through the distance, carefully scanning every object that seemed to have life or motion.

The first clergyman I there heard preach was Mr. Gano, father of the late General Gano of this city, then a captain and one of the earliest settlers of Columbia.[11] Never shall I forget that holy and venerable man, with locks white with years, as with a voice tremulous with age he ably expounded the word of truth and affectionately encouraged penitent sinners to hope in the Divine forgiveness, from the words of Job, "O that I knew where I might find Him! that I might come even to His seat! I would order my cause before Him, and fill my mouth with arguments." He has long since gone to reap the reward of them "that turn many to righteousness," and most of those once his hearers are dwellers in that land whence they shall never emigrate. Often, too, as I rest quietly in a comfortable dwelling or sit at a table crowned with plenty, possessing not only every necessary, but some of the luxuries of life, I think of the hardships of the early settlers of the West; and contrasting their perils and privations with the security and plenty of the present day, mentally exclaim with the Psalmist: "The lines are fallen unto us in pleasant places; yea, we have a goodly heritage." My wife, who now sits beside me, and whose parents settled at Marietta in the spring of 1790, says that so great in that summer was the scarcity of breadstuffs that her mother was obliged to send her children from the house while she prepared bread for her boarders, who by some fortunate circumstance had obtained a bushel of corn meal; and I have often heard that in the Miami settlements the same summer many, while planting and tending their crops were confined wholly to boiled corn as a substitute for bread; and sometimes, destitute even of that, used in its stead a sweet bulbous root, called bear grass.

I well recollect that in 1791 so scarce and dear was flour that the little that could be afforded in families was laid by to be used only in sickness, or for the entertainment of friends; and although corn was then abundant, there was but one mill (Wickerham's), a floating mill on the Little Miami, near where Turpin's now stands. Built in a small flatboat tied to the bank, its wheel turning slowly with the natural current running between the flat and a small pirogue anchored in the stream, and on which one end of its shaft rested, and having only one pair of small stones it was at best barely sufficient to supply meal for the inhabitants of Columbia and the neighboring families; and sometimes from low water

---

[11]The father was Rev. Stephen Gano, founder of the Baptist church at Columbia, whose church building is sometimes said to have been the first in the state of Ohio. The son was Major-General John S. Gano, who served with William Henry Harrison in the northwestern wars of this period. On the occasion of the celebration of the forty-fifth anniversary of the settling of Cincinnati, December 26, 1833, General Harrison paid an eloquent tribute to the soldierly and other virtues of General Gano.

and other unfavorable circumstances it was of little use, so that we were obliged to supply the deficiency from hand mills, a most laborious mode of grinding.

The winter of 1791–92 was followed by an early and delightful spring; indeed, I have often thought that our first western winters were much milder, our springs earlier, and our autumns longer than they are now. On the last of February some of the trees were putting forth their foliage; in March the red bud, the hawthorn, and the dogwood, in full bloom, checkered the hills, displaying their beautiful colors of rose and lily; and in April the ground was covered with mayapple, bloodroot, ginseng, violets, and a great variety of herbs and flowers. Flocks of parroquets were seen, decked in their rich plumage of green and gold. Birds of various species and of every hue were flitting from tree to tree, and the beautiful redbird and the untaught songster of the West made the woods vocal with their melody. Now might be heard the plaintive wail of the dove, and now the rumbling drum of the partridge or the loud gobble of the turkey. Here might be seen the clumsy bear, doggedly moving off, or urged by pursuit into a laboring gallop, retreating to his citadel in the top of some lofty tree; or, approached suddenly, raising himself erect in the attitude of defense facing his enemy, and waiting his approach; there the timid deer, watchfully resting or cautiously feeding, or aroused from his thicket gracefully bounding off, then stopping, erecting his stately head, and for a moment gazing around or snuffing the air to ascertain his enemy, instantly springing off, clearing logs and bushes at a bound and soon distancing his pursuers.

It seemed an earthly paradise; and but for apprehension of the wily copperhead, who lay silently coiled among the leaves or beneath the plants waiting to strike his victim; the horrid rattlesnake, who, more chivalrous, however, with head erect amidst his ample folds, prepared to dart upon his foe, generously, with the loud noise of his rattle, apprised him of his danger; and the still more fearful and insidious savage, who, crawling upon the ground or noiselessly approaching behind trees and thickets, sped the deadly shaft or fatal bullet, you might have fancied you were in the confines of Eden or the borders of Elysium.

At this delightful season the inhabitants of our village went forth to their labor, inclosing their fields which the spring flood had opened, tilling their ground, and planting their corn for their next year's sustenance. I said went forth, for their principal cornfield was distant from Columbia about one and a half miles east, and adjoining the extensive plain on which the town stood. That large tract of alluvial ground, still known by the name of Turkey Bottom, and which, lying about fifteen feet below the adjoining plain and annually overflowed, is yet very fertile, was laid off into lots of five acres each and owned by the inhabitants of Columbia; some possessing one, and others two or more lots, and to save labor, was enclosed with one fence.

Here the men generally worked in companies, exchanging labor, or in adjoining fields, with their firearms near them, and in case of an attack ready to unite for their common defense. Here their usual annual crop of corn from ground very ordinarily cultivated was eighty bushels per acre; and some lots, well-tilled, produced a hundred, and in very favorable seasons a hundred and ten bushels to the acre. An inhabitant of New England, New Jersey, or some portions of Maryland would scarcely think it credible that in hills four feet apart were four or five stalks, one and a half inches in diameter and fifteen feet in height, bearing each two or three ears of corn, of which some were so far from the ground that to pull them an ordinary man was obliged to stand on tiptoe. Small as I then was I drove the oxen while my father, followed by the corn dressers, guided the plow between the rows; for having lost our horses we were obliged to substitute cattle; which, however, connected by a long yoke having the draft near to one of them and permitting each to walk in a separate row, fully supplied the place of a horse.

Well do I recollect with what alacrity I performed my labor on the promise of my father that I should spend the approaching Fourth of July at Fort Washington; and well do I remember with what gayety and high expectations of coming pleasure I left home to realize those expectations. It was on the afternoon of the third of July, 1792, in company with my sisters and several ladies of Columbia, and some officers who had arrived there on the morning of that day for the express purpose of conveying them to Fort Washington to partake of a dinner to be given by the officers and followed with a ball on the evening of the Fourth. We left the shore in front of my father's dwelling in a fine barge rowed by eight soldiers, and were soon descending with the rapid current of the river at the rate of six miles an hour.

The scenery of the Ohio between Columbia and Cincinnati was in those days truly romantic: scarcely a tree had been cut on either side between the mouth of the Crawfish and that of Deer Creek, a distance of more than four miles. The sand-bar now extending from its left bank opposite to Sportmen's Hall was then a small island, between which and the Kentucky shore was a narrow channel with sufficient depth of water for the passage of boats. The upper and lower points of this island were bare, but its center, embracing about four acres, was covered with small cottonwood and surrounded by willows extending along its sides almost down to the water's edge. The right bank of the river, crowned with its lofty hills, now gradually ascending and now rising abruptly to their summits and forming a vast amphitheater, was from Columbia, extending down about two miles, very steep, and covered with trees quite down to the beach. From thence, nearly opposite the foot of the island, its ascent became more gradual, and for two miles farther down, bordering the tall trees with which it was covered, was a thick growth of willows through which in many places it was difficult to penetrate. Below this the beach was wide and stony, with only here and there a small tuft of willows, while the wood on the side and on the top of the bank was more open. Not far from this bank, and near the line of the present turnpike, was a narrow road leading from Columbia to Cincinnati, just wide enough for the passage of a wagon, which, winding around the point of the hill above Deer Creek, descended northwardly about four hundred feet, and crossing that creek in a southerly direction, ascending gradually its western bank, led along the ground, now Symmes Street, directly toward Fort Washington, and diverging at the intersection of Lawrence Street to the right and left of the fort, entered the town. I have been thus particular in describing the river between Columbia and Cincinnati, not only that those who now see it may have some idea of its former appearance, but that the reader may better understand the narrative that follows.

Scarcely an hour, enlivened by conversation, had elapsed from the time we left Columbia before we landed on the shore in front of the garrison and, ascending the bank, in a few minutes entered Fort Washington.

The morning of the Fourth was ushered in by the discharge of thirteen rounds from the cannon of the fort; at twelve the firing was repeated, and the troops under arms performed various evolutions; at dinner, as usual, the toasts were followed by the discharge of artillery; at dusk there was a brilliant exhibition of fireworks; and at night, if not a splendid, yet in the opinion of those present, a very agreeable and sprightly ball. The two succeeding days were spent by me in various amusements; but having exhausted these and grown tired of play I became restless and uneasy, and determining to return home, with all the inconsiderateness of childhood (for I was not then eleven years old) I secretly left the garrison, whose first knowledge of my absence was the report of my capture.

Reaching the bank in front of the fort about three o'clock on the afternoon of the seventh, I found a canoe with four persons on board bound for Columbia, just about to push off from the shore. Discovering one of them to be an acquaintance I hailed them, requesting them to take me on board; which request, after a few moments' consultation, they complied with. The canoe, which was small, narrow, and quite unsteady, had proceeded only a few rods above the mouth of Deer Creek when one of the men, much intoxicated, having made several lurches on both sides, at length tumbling overboard and nearly overset-ting us, after a few awkward flounces reached the shore. Not knowing how to swim and being afraid to continue in the canoe, I prevailed on the remaining men to set me on shore; when, after a few minutes, leaving the drunken man sitting on the bank we proceeded toward Columbia. In the bow of the canoe stood Mr. Jacob Light, who with a pole aided in propelling it; in the stern, a stranger, a swarthy, athletic man, with thick, black, bushy hair, sat with a paddle, which he some-times used as an oar and at others as a rudder; and in the bottom of its center sat Mrs. Coleman, then an old woman of sixty. For myself, I walked along the beach a little below the canoe, now listening to the merry conversation of my companions and now amusing myself by skimming small flat stones over the surface of the water.

About a mile above the mouth of Deer Creek a canoe which we had discovered some time before descending the middle of the river, having on board some market people and a woman whose child cried loudly and incessantly, passed us, and elicited from the old lady, as is common in such cases, some remarks on the government of children. We had rounded the point of a small cove less than a mile below the foot of the island and proceeded a few hundred yards along the close willows, here bordering the beach at about two rods' distance from the water, when the stranger in the stern of the canoe, looking back and discovering the drunken man staggering along the shore nearly a mile below us, re-marked with an oath that he would be "bait for the Indians." Scarcely had he spoken and resumed his labor, for a few moments suspended, when turning my eyes from the drunken man to the men in the canoe I saw Mr. Light spring suddenly into the river and the stranger at the stern falling over toward the shore. In the next moment, hearing the sharp crack of two rifles in instant succession and looking toward the willows about two rods above me, I saw through the thick smoke of their guns two Indians, with faces black as midnight, rushing toward the canoe.

Never shall I forget my feelings at that moment. For an instant I stood motionless and my brief reflection in that moment, as I involuntarily drew down my head between my shoulders, was: I have made some narrow escapes but now death is inevitable. One Indian was now within ten feet of me; in his right hand was the uplifted tomahawk and in his left the naked scalping knife. Instantly as on wheeling, I ran toward the water, hoping to reach the canoe and push out into the river; he passed above me down to the shore, near which I arrived just at the moment when, striking his tomahawk into the head of the unfortunate stranger, seizing him by the hair, passing his knife quickly around his scalp and tearing it violently off, he held it up for a moment with fiendish exultation. Finding I could not gain the canoe which by this time had got out into the current, turning from the heart-sickening sight of the mangled man, and dreading every moment a similar fate, I next attempted to run down the river in the vain hope of escaping; but I had not proceeded ten steps when the other Indian, discovering my design, easily headed me. Instead, however, of seizing me violently, approaching within a few feet he extended to me his hand in token of peace. I took it, and from what I had heard of the character and customs of the Indians feeling assured of present safety, became at once calm.

The whole of these events did not occupy more than thirty seconds. The Indians had been on the hill in quest of horses, when hearing the loud crying of the child in the canoe that about ten minutes before had passed us, they came down to the bank of the river thinking they might have an opportunity of effecting some mischief. Arriving too late to injure those in that canoe and discovering ours about a quarter of a mile below, the Indians determined to wait our approach; and having planned to kill the men and women and take me a prisoner, concealed themselves behind a large log among the willows, whence, as we came nearly opposite, they made their attack.

I had time only to cast a brief glance at the shocking scene before me; to see Mr. Light, who, although wounded in the left arm, was with his right swimming out into the river, about a hundred yards from shore; the dead body of the stranger lying just in the edge of the water; Mrs. Coleman about two rods out in the river, her clothes spread over the water and with her head near its surface, apparently floating, and the desolate canoe slowly descending with the current, when the Indian who had taken me prisoner and who still held my hand led me off; and followed by his companion, whose tomahawk was extended almost over my head, soon began to climb the high hill bordering the Ohio.

Crossing the road a short distance we stopped a few moments on the hillside; the Indians, casting their keen glances around them and listening intently as if hearing some sound indicative of danger, then, apparently satisfied that they were undiscovered, resumed their retreat and quickly gaining the top of the hill, ran off in a northerly direction at the height of my speed, one of them still holding me by my hand, the other following with his uplifted tomahawk.

Having run, as I judged, about four miles, discovering my feet bare (for I had soon after leaving Cincinnati thrown my shoes into the canoe) my conductor, whom I now regarded as my master, supplied me with a pair of moccasins and seemed much pleased when in return for them I gave him my pocket handkerchief, which he received as a mark of gratitude. To the other Indian, who had now put his tomahawk in his belt, fearing that I might have excited his jealousy I presented my hat, which at first as worthless he dashed on the ground; then, instantly picking it up, thinking, no doubt, it might direct pursuit, carried it in his hand until evening when he burned it. Relaxing our speed (although the long strides of the Indians kept me in a continual trot) and still pursuing a northerly course, about an hour before sunset, descending a high hill, we reached a small stream running in a westerly direction, and which I have since believed to be the rivulet and hill adjoining Sharon. Entering this stream we waded up it about half a mile, the leading Indian directing me to step in his track while the other followed treading in mine; then leaving it and traveling about a mile farther north, encamped at sunset on a low point of thick underwood near a rivulet.

Here, while one Indian kindled a fire the other went in pursuit of game, and soon returned with a raccoon, which he had killed with his rifle, proceeded to dress it by singeing off the hair, then dividing it, broiled it on the fire. The Indians ate voraciously, but being exceedingly weary I could eat very little; besides I had just witnessed a most sickening scene, calculated for a time to destroy all relish for food. While my captor was dressing the raccoon for supper I had seen the other Indian, whom I shall now call by his name, Wawpawmawquaw or White Loon, drawing from its sheath his large brass-handled knife and cutting off the limb of a small grub near the body, take from his bullet pouch the black scalp recently torn from the head of the unfortunate white man, and cutting a small hole near its edge and hanging it on the stump of the severed limb deliberately and carefully scrape off the thick fat; then, forming a small hoop about six inches in diameter, with a thread of deer's sinew stretch the scalp within it as if he had been preparing to dry the skin of an animal. Having finished their meal the Indians prepared for rest; first tying the middle of a cord around my neck and extending its ends around my wrists separately, they spread a blanket on the ground and ordered me to lie down; then, lying down on each side of me, passing the ends of the cord under their bodies and covering themselves with the remaining blanket, soon sunk into a profound sleep.

For some time I lay ruminating on the sad events of the past day, my mind now filled with fearful apprehensions of the future and now "stung with the thought of home," to which I feared I should never return. Here, as I thought of my beloved parents and affectionate sisters and felt for the moment that I should never again behold them, tears of bitter regret flowed plentifully, and scarcely could I repress my sobs; then, as for a moment a ray of hope shone through the gloom, my soul became more tranquil and I began to revolve in my mind the means and the probabilities of escape; overcome at length with fatigue, in deep sleep I soon forgot all my sorrows.

CHAPTER IV

To ME IT has ever seemed almost incredible that Mrs. Coleman, after jumping out of the canoe into the river, should have floated quite down to Cincinnati, and there, being taken out of the water, have communicated the bloody event of that day and the news of my captivity; but the fact has been often declared by herself and asserted by others of undoubted veracity, some of whom it is said had aided in saving her. [12] I have been told, however, that the first news of my captivity was communicated by Mr. Light, who on seeing the Indians retreat swam to the shore, and making the best of his way to Fort Washington reported the fact. The commanding officer immediately dispatched an express to my father, announcing the painful occurrence and proposing to send out a small force of regulars. While the news was spreading, a number of the inhabitants of Columbia soon assembled, prepared and anxious to pursue the Indians; but my father, apprehending that finding themselves pursued and unable to carry me off, the Indians would instantly kill me, returned by the express a request that no troops should be sent after them; then with some difficulty dissuading his neighbors from their purposed pursuit, obtained the promise that they would proceed no farther than the spot where the dead man still lay, and where I was taken prisoner.

---

[12]The apparent incredibility of Mrs. Coleman's exploit as here set forth was recognized by other contemporaries than Spencer. A note in the historical sketch published in the *Cincinnati Directory* for 1819, after stating that without any exertion on her part Mrs. Coleman floated between one and two miles, offers this explanation: "It is supposed she was borne up by her dress, which according to the fashion of that time, consisted of a stuffed quilt and other buoyant robes." In the Draper Mss. of the Wisconsin Historical Library a somewhat more prosaic account of Mrs. Coleman's feat is given. It represents that after drifting about 100 yards she was caught on a snag, from which predicament she was rescued by some of her Columbia neighbors. This story was told to Dr. Draper in 1839 by an old resident of Columbia.

To describe the feelings of my parents when the news of my captivity reached them would for me be impossible. To be bereaved of an only son, and the youngest of a once numerous family of whom but six were living, would by death under ordinary circumstances have been a severe affliction. Had I been found dead, inhumanly scalped and mangled, on the beach by the side of my unfortunate companion, the shock though powerful would have gradually subsided, and the violence of grief would with time have abated; but that I should be carried away captive by the Indians, the cruel, barbarous savages, was to my parents and especially to my mother almost insupportable. Often, when she thought of me, she fancied she saw me fainting with fatigue or famishing with hunger or pining with disease; and sometimes her terrified imagination represented me falling by the knife or sinking under the stroke of the tomahawk or expiring at the stake in the flames, under the most cruel tortures. Nor was she relieved from these distressing apprehensions and this painful state of suspense until some time in November following my captivity, when certain information was received from the commanding officer at Post Vincennes that I was then living, and had been seen at the Indian village near the mouth of Auglaize only a few weeks before by the late Captain Wells (Indian agent, who was killed by the Indians at the capture of Chicago, in the late war with Great Britain), then a prisoner at large among the Indians. [13]

With the dawn of the morning of the eighth of July the Indians awoke, and untying the cord with which I was bound we all arose. Our scanty breakfast was soon made from the remains of the raccoon which had furnished our supper; our baggage, consisting of two blankets, a bridle, a cord, and a scalp was shouldered, the priming of the rifles was examined, and before the sun rose we were marching in single file, my master in front, myself in the center, and the White Loon bringing up the rear, in the direct course of the Shawnee villages. The morning of

---

[13]Captain William Wells, son of a prominent Kentucky family, was, like Spencer, carried into captivity as a boy by the Indians. Unlike Spencer, however, Wells was not rescued therefrom. He grew up among the Indians, married a daughter of the noted chief, Little Turtle, and became noted for his prowess as a warrior. He took part in St. Clair's defeat, and there is no inherent improbability in the story that he slew several of the Americans on this occasion. Not long after, however, he decided to abandon his Indian life and rejoin his native race. His knowledge of the Indians made him a valuable addition to the white ranks, and he served as chief of scouts in Wayne's campaign of 1794. Notwithstanding his desertion of them, the red men continued to hold him in esteem, and at the Treaty of Greenville which closed this period of Indian warfare the Miami especially requested that Wells be sent among them as Indian agent. Thereafter his home was at Fort Wayne until he met his death in 1812 in a vain effort to rescue the doomed Fort Dearborn garrison from impending destruction. For a fuller account of Wells' career and death, see the editor's *Chicago and the Old Northwest*, 224–28.

this day was very pleasant: the sky was clear and the air balmy and refreshing; the ground, less broken and hilly, was covered with verdure; the tall woods through which we passed were beautiful, and but for the condition in which I was, a captive whose every step bore him farther from friends and home, I should have been delighted. As it was, however, my mind by degrees became more cheerful and my spirits began to resume their native elasticity.

About noon this day, passing along the east side of a hill beyond which there appeared to be a large opening, the Indians moved cautiously, half bent and with trailed rifles. Proceeding about half a mile we halted in a deep ravine, when White Loon, taking the bridle and pursuing a westerly course down the hollow, soon disappeared. In about ten minutes, however, he returned, mounted on a fine cream-colored horse which he had just stolen, and taking me up behind him trotted off several miles, the other Indian following, until coming to a thick undergrowth we slackened our pace into a brisk walk. Here we found a faint trace which, pursuing a few miles, led us into a plain path which I afterwards learned was the Indians' war path.

The Indians seemed highly pleased with their late acquisition, riding by turns the spirited animal, and, occasionally taking me behind them, greatly relieved me from fatigue. But, alas! how uncertain are the comforts of this world! About the middle of the afternoon the horse suddenly became dull and seemingly sullen, so that with difficulty he could be urged forward. At length he stopped short, when in vain did the White Loon on foot apply the hickory: the horse only stood and kicked. In vain did the other Indian, dismounting, endeavor to lead him forward; he would proceed no farther. He had been violently attacked with either bots or colic, and now lying suddenly began to roll and groan, sometimes struggling with every limb and sometimes dashing his head against the ground. The Indians stood over him, now beating him severely and now talking to him in Indian as if expostulating with him or threatening him with vengeance in case of his remaining stubborn; at length my master, seizing his rifle as if to shoot him, began in broken English to curse him, and after loading the poor animal with all the opprobrious epithets he could think of, left him lying in the path.

We encamped this evening about sunset in a low rich bottom near a beautiful stream; where having made a fire and roasted part of a young fawn which White Loon a few minutes before had killed, we ate a very hearty supper, though without salt or bread, neither of which did we taste until we arrived at the Indian villages. After supper, taking a small piece of tobacco and cutting it fine by passing the edge of his knife between his forefinger and thumb, receiving it as thus prepared into the palm of his left hand, the White Loon with great solemnity and apparent devotion sprinkled a few grains of it on the coals, an offering, as I afterwards understood, to the Great Spirit, moving his lips as if uttering some petition; then, mingling the residue with some dried sumach leaves which he drew from his bullet pouch and filling the bowl of his tomahawk, serving as a pipe, first smoked a few whiffs, then handed the pipe to his companion, who also smoking a few minutes returned it; the Indians thus alternately puffing until the tobacco was consumed, frequently filling their mouths with smoke and forcing it through their nostrils, closing their brief use of the pipe with a peculiar suck of the breath and a slight grinding of the teeth. The day had been remarkably fine; we had traveled with short intermissions from early dawn until sunset, a distance of at least forty miles; and very weary, myself at least, we lay down before our fire under a spreading beech and soon fell into a profound sleep.

But we had slept only a few hours when we were awakened by the roar of a tremendous hurricane passing only a few rods north of us, prostrating the trees with a terrible crash and carrying devastation in its broad track. Over our heads the thunders broke with deafening peals and the lightnings seemed a constant sheet of flame, while from the black dense cloud that was furiously sweeping eastward it sent its vivid bolts athwart and onward, passing the storm with the rapidity of thought. I had sprung from the ground and, gazing on the awful scene, stood motionless with terror. I feared that the "great day of God's wrath was come," and felt that I was not "able to stand"; I vowed to God that if he would spare me I would dedicate to him my future life; but alas! no sooner had the fury of the storm passed and the thunder, now distant, ceased to terrify me, than my vows to God were forgotten and the thoughts of the great white throne were banished. Expecting every moment to perish, I stood for some minutes unconscious of the presence of a human being; but my terror a little subsiding, looking at the Indians who were standing near me I saw them perfectly calm, apparently insensible of danger, gazing with a sort of delighted wonder; and frequently, as from the dense cloud shot some more vivid bolt with more deafening peal, expressing their admiration with their customary exclamation, Wawhaugh! waugh!

On the morning of the ninth the sun rose brightly above the cloudless horizon and shone upon a sky as clear and beautiful as if it had never been darkened by clouds or torn by tempests; and but for the bent treetops above us, the fallen branches around us, and the widespread devastation before us, one would scarcely have believed that in the heavens now so bright and tranquil, desolation and terror had so lately held their empire. Breakfasting early, we pursued our journey; but our progress for the first half hour was slow and very difficult, having sometimes to climb over the large bodies of the fallen trees, or to wind around their uptorn roots; and sometimes to creep through their tops, interwoven with the underwood. One who has never seen the effects of a tornado can have but a faint idea of its power and operation. Here, for at least a quarter of a mile in width and many miles in length not a tree had been able to withstand its force; not only were the largest trees torn up by the roots, but many one and even two feet in diameter were twisted off, some near to the ground and others ten or twenty feet from it, apparently with as much ease as a man would break off a slender twig.

Passing at length the fallen trees and traveling on a few hours, on hearing the sound of a bell we halted not far from a small opening on our left. Here Wawpawmawquaw left us, again taking a westerly direction, and in about half an hour returned with an old black horse, probably a packhorse belonging to the army, that had given out and afterwards strayed off. Suspended from his neck by a broad leather strap was a large bell, which was now stuffed with grass to prevent its tinkling. This horse, though very far inferior to the one we had lost, was esteemed a valuable acquisition, particularly by me; for my feet had now become sore from walking, and I was delighted with the opportunity of relief which riding afforded. Mounted upon the old horse, a natural pacer, I now rode very pleasantly, enjoying the comfort thus accidentally afforded me without interruption, for the Indians seemed not at all disposed to share it with me.

Having halted at noon and taken some refreshment we traveled on until about six o'clock, when passing along the side of a ridge into a low bottom, we stopped on the south bank of a beautiful stream (which I have since been told by the White Loon is Buck Creek) in the edge of a grove covering both banks of the stream, skirting on one side a small natural meadow of a few acres and on the other a large prairie extending a mile or two north and west. Here, determined to remain until the next day, the Indians proceeded to hopple the horse, and unstopping his bell turned him out to graze. Next, intending to secure me, they ordered me to sit down with my back against a small tree; then taking their cord, tying it first to the tree, passing it around my neck, and then with a knot around my wrists separately, extending my arms obliquely on each side they fastened one end of it to a stake driven into the ground and the other to a root in the bank of the stream; then placing a large piece of bark over me to shelter me from the sun, went out to hunt.

Being left alone, my thoughts alternately occupied with tender recollections of my home and a painful consciousness of my wretched condition, sometimes revolving in my mind the probability of escape, then rejecting the thought as chimerical, an hour had passed away. I now began to think seriously of making my escape and after a few minutes determined if possible to effect it. Being a firm believer in an overruling Providence and in the concern of God for the welfare of his creatures, I first addressed myself to Him and never did I utter a more sincere and fervent prayer, supplicating His mercy and imploring His aid, and promising that if He would deliver me from the hands of the savages and restore me to my beloved parents I would serve Him the residue of my days "in truth with all my heart." Believing, too, in the use of means, I immediately began to exert my own powers. Seizing the cord with which I was bound I first pulled it violently with my right hand, attempting to break it or detach it from the root to which it was fastened; failing in this effort I next laid hold of it with my left, endeavoring to pull down the stake to which it was tied. While trying to effect this, looking at the stake over my left hand I discovered that the cord was tied on the outside of the cuff of my sleeve and, making the effort, succeeded in drawing my arm through it; then, with the aid of my left disengaging my right hand in the same way, I soon set myself entirely free.

Picking up the bridle and thrusting in my bosom a small piece of flyblown deer's meat as provision for my journey, I soon found, bridled, and unhoppled the old horse; and mounting on his back and using the hopples (a cord of twisted bark) in place of a whip set off for home. From the report of their rifles, which I had heard only a few minutes before, I judged that the Indians were about a mile off in a southwesterly direction, and that I should easily return along the path we had traveled, unperceived; for considerate for a child as I might have been, the thoughts of home so engrossed my mind that the probability and even certainty of pursuit did not enter into my calculations, and I thought that if I could only get a few miles from the camp undiscovered I should be safe. Unfortunately, as it then seemed, I could not urge the horse beyond a moderate pace. Whipping him with the hopples until I was tired, I threw them down in the path and supplied their place with a switch; but with all my exertions, striking with my heels, jerking with the bridle, and applying the switch simultaneously, I could not force him into a trot. The sun when I left the camp was about an hour high, and as I traveled steadily until sunset I had probably proceeded three or four miles when, concluding to halt for the night, I dismounted from the horse and bending a small twig by the side of the path in a direction toward home, I led him a few hundred yards directly off from the trace, up a gentle slope of woodland into a very close thicket of small sassafras, and securing him with the bridle went in search of a lodging place.

About sixty yards south of the thicket, finding a large fallen tree facing the path and having near its roots a hollow forming a shelter, I determined to lodge under it; but being very hungry and having no provisions for my journey saving a small piece of meat, which I thought I should more need on the morrow, I concluded to make my evening's meal on raspberries, which grew here in great abundance. Straying from bush to bush, eagerly picking and eating to satisfy my hunger, I paid little attention to my course; when, having eaten sufficiently, I turned, as I thought, toward my lodging place, but found after walking some time that I was completely lost. I now felt greatly alarmed; I ran about in every direction seeking the thicket where I had tied the horse, and terrified at the thought of perishing in the wilderness, regretted for a moment my attempt to escape. Happily, however, after wandering about for some time I found the log, and lying down under it, pillowing my head on some leaves which I scraped together and covered with my jacket, and devoutly thanking God for saving me from the horror of losing myself and starving in the wilderness and for all His kindness thus far, composed myself to rest.

CHAPTER V

THE SUN HAD set with the promise of a fair morrow; evening, mild and calm, had followed him; the soft twilight, gradually deepening, was fast merging into night; the birds had chanted their vesper hymn and a deep and universal stillness reigned. I felt that I was alone in the midst of a vast wilderness, exposed to prowling wolves and deadly panthers, and my heart for a moment sank within me from a sense of my utter helplessness and of my inability to oppose even the barrier of a fire between me and destruction; then the thought of home and the hope of reaching it in safety banished my fears and inspired me with fresh courage. I had lain thus but a few minutes, now closing my eyes to sleep and now opening them upon the spreading tree tops, or stars faintly glimmering through their branches, when I was suddenly aroused by the cracking of bushes and a noise like that from quick strokes on the ground, and looking toward the path saw a herd of deer bounding through the woods and swiftly approaching me. Presently one of them sprang over the log under which I lay; the others, leaping between me and the thicket where I had tied the horse, were in the next moment out of sight.

Scarcely had I lain down again, when, hearing a rustling among the bushes at a short distance from me, I raised myself upon my elbow to ascertain the cause; but words cannot express my feelings nor describe my consternation and dismay when, looking through an opening between the roots of the fallen tree under which I lay, I saw the two Indians whom I had left enter the thicket. Advancing immediately to the horse and laying hold of his bridle, they stood a few moments, looking through the small opening in the thicket facing the spot where I lay, in different directions evidently endeavoring to discover me. I had by this time partially recovered my self-possession, and fearing that if I waited for them to find me they would tomahawk me where I lay, determined at once to return to them. Instantly springing up and putting on my jacket, I ran to the thicket and with the mingled fear of deserved punishment and the slight hope of impunity uttered the truly childlike excuse, "I have been out picking raspberries."

Methinks I can now see the horrible savage grinding his teeth with rage, and with a look of fiendish malice that almost froze my blood raise his rifle to his shoulder intending to shoot me. Were my mother's prayers now ascending before the Throne? Was my father now supplicating protection for his lost son? Or had the Father of Mercies said, "Lay not thine hand upon the lad"? At that moment the generous Wawpawmawquaw interposed, and throwing up the muzzle of the nearly leveled rifle, saved my life. A brief altercation and then a few moments' earnest conversation ensued, after which, setting down their rifles and cutting large switches from the thicket, they beat me severely on my head and shoulders until their whips were literally "used up." I bore their beating, however, with the firmness of an Indian; never once complaining nor entreating remission, but not daring to make further resistance than to throw up my arms to protect my head. Often since have I felt thankful that there were none other than sassafras bushes near; for had the Indians thus beaten me with hickory or oak they would certainly have killed me. Having wearied themselves in punishing me and having told me by signs which I could not misunderstand that if again I should attempt to escape they would certainly kill and scalp me, we set out for our camp, the White Loon in front leading me by the hand and the other Indian following on the horse, until we reached the path, when we proceeded along it in single file.

If at any time I flagged a little, falling too far behind the leading Indian, the cruel savage behind me goaded me with a stick or strove to ride over me; and after proceeding about two miles, discovering in the path the bark hopples I had thrown down, he sprang from the horse and picking them up inflicted many severe blows with them on my head and shoulders. Weary and faint, I rejoiced when at last we reached the camp; but my satisfaction was momentary only, for without stopping even to secure the horse the Indians proceeded to tie me. Passing a cord around my elbows they drew them together behind my back so closely as to almost dislocate my shoulders; then tying my wrists so tightly as nearly to prevent the circulation of the blood in my hands, they fastened the ends of the cord to a forked stake driven into the ground. I had often, as I thought, suffered not a little, but my sufferings this night were extreme; I could not lie down, and to sleep was impossible; my head, bruised and swollen, pained me exceedingly, but this was trivial when compared with the torture I suffered from the violent straining of my arms behind my back; my ribs seemed every moment as though they would separate from my breast, and my shoulder blades felt as if they would separate from my body. Forgetting the late signal instances of divine interposition, I murmured against God, and in the bitterness of my soul longed for death.

The night seemed as if it would never end; but at length the day dawned and gratefully did I hail the cheerful sunrise, when the Indians, having eaten their breakfast and being ready to march, came and unbinding me relieved me from the severity of suffering. Immediately fording Buck Creek (the eastern branch of Mad River), here about thirty feet wide and swelled by the late rain, rising above my waist, we passed on in a northwesterly direction through the eastern side of a prairie, near to a high woodland, about a mile and a half, and crossing Mad River (an important branch of the Great Miami) at a broad ford sixty feet wide, ascended a high bank matted with blue grass, covered with raspberry bushes and plum trees, and exhibiting the appearance of having been once the site of an Indian village. Here, the Indians stopping a few minutes to adjust their blankets and make a pair of bark stirrups, I availed myself of the opportunity to breakfast on the raspberries, which were abundant.

Traveling on in a northwest course through open woods, over high rolling ground, about noon we descended into a rich bottom and halted on the bank of a small creek near a fine spring. Distant from this spot a few rods was a very large sycamore, hollow at the bottom and having on the side facing us an opening about six feet high, barricaded below with logs covered with brush. To this tree the Indians immediately proceeded, and removing the brush from before it and looking into its hollow for a moment, returned to the spring, where making a fire and roasting some squirrels which they had killed in the morning they made their dinner.

I had eaten nothing but raspberries for the last twenty-four hours; I was very hungry; yet the Indians offered me no food. I thought of their late cruel treatment of me and of their continued inhumanity. I looked at the opening of the hollow sycamore, which appeared black within as if it had been burned, and suddenly was seized with the apprehension that they there intended to burn me. Weak and faint from want of rest, of food, and from the debilitating effects of a severe dysentery with which I had been seized in the morning; stiff and sore from beating and from confinement, my feet swelled from walking and my legs torn with briars, I was truly an object of pity. I sat with my back toward the Indians ruminating on my wretched condition and gloomy prospects, now begging for death to release me from my sufferings and now shrinking from the thought of its pain, its terrors, and above all from that eternity beyond it for which I felt that I was wholly unprepared. Soon, however, I found relief in a flood of tears, which I carefully concealed from the Indians, and washing my face and bathing my throbbing temples at the brook strove to assume the semblance of cheerfulness. The Indians now leading the horse out to the hollow sycamore and removing the logs from before its opening, I soon discovered the cause of their late haste to examine it, and with that discovery dismissed my foolish apprehensions. It is worthy of remark that in their villages the Indians use neither bolts nor locks, and that when they leave for a time their cabins, either empty or with any articles in them, a log placed against its door affords ample protection to its contents and abundant evidence of the right of possession in its owner; a right seldom if ever violated, even by the most worthless among them. The same respect is paid, even in the wilderness, to property known or believed to belong to Indians of the same tribe or to those of other tribes at peace with them.

If discovered, their property here had remained inviolate; and now, taking from within the hollow tree an old blanket and pack saddle and fastening them upon the horse's back, the Indians next brought out two large packs of deer skins of equal size, neatly folded and firmly tied together, and connecting them with tugs of rawhide and placing them on the saddle so that they hung about half way down his sides, made them fast with a cord; then securing between the packs a small brass kettle, made to contain about two gallons and completing the contents of the tree, we took up our line of march. Providing me with a switch and placing me next to the horse, Wawpawmawquaw followed, ordering me to urge him forward, and whenever he lagged touching me with his whipping stick and pointing to the lazy animal would cry, "Howh caucheeh!" meaning that I should quicken his gait. This employment gave me a little excitement and helped to rouse me from a lethargy produced by sickness and weariness; but from which nothing could have effectually quickened me, save the certain expectation of death the moment that from any cause I should be unable to proceed.

From the conduct of the Indians I suspected, what I afterwards found to be the fact, that after my late attempt to escape from them I became the property of Wawpawmawquaw by purchase from the other Indian, who now exercised no control over me. This gave me some comfort, as my former master (a Shawnee), besides being an ugly-looking fellow and having something sinister in his countenance, evidenced a very cruel and savage disposition and withal great meanness and selfishness; and, indeed, to me seemed destitute of every manly feeling; while Wawpawmawquaw (the son of a Mohawk chief, now from the almost utter extinction of his nation united with the Shawnees), though in battle fierce as brave, was at other times (for a savage) humane and benevolent. His person, a little above the middle size, was well formed, combining activity with strength; his face was fine, his countenance open and intelligent, and his bearing noble and manly. True, like all Indians, under deep wrongs he was vindictive; but while some of his nation, deserting its ranks, fought on the side of its oppressors, disdaining to aid his natural enemies to crush the remnant of his race, he remained unchangeable in his opposition to the "pale face," bravely resisting their continued aggressions so long as there appeared to be the slightest hope of preventing their further encroachment; then yielding to the power of circumstances, submitting calmly to his fate.

Having traveled since morning about thirty miles, two hours before sunset we forded a large stream (then to me waist high) to which Wawpawmawquaw, pointing, said, "Miami"; and which from its course here, a little north of west, from its long rapid, and from the appearance of the banks on both sides, I have since been satisfied that we crossed about two miles above Sidney. We encamped in the evening about six miles beyond the Miami at a small creek; where, for the first time in thirty-six hours making a hearty meal, I slept quietly through the night and awoke in the morning greatly refreshed.

In the course of a few hours' traveling this morning, crossing a great many small branches running in various directions and then passing through a very extensive prairie, we came to a stream running northwardly, and following its course until noon halted by the side of a small rivulet. Having no provisions Wawpawmawquaw went to hunt some, but soon returned unsuccessful. Just at this time a large hawk flying over our heads with a snake in its talons and alighting on a tree a short distance from us was brought down with the rifle, and being dressed by plucking out the larger and singeing off the smaller feathers, and then boiled in our brass kettle with a quantity of milkweed, in about half an hour furnished us a dinner of flesh, soup, and greens. Even the Indians ate sparingly; for myself, though hungry, I found the hawk so tough and strong that I could eat but a few mouthfuls; as for the soup and greens, without salt the taste was not only insipid, but sickening.

About the middle of the afternoon we met a small company of Indian hunters, the first human beings we had seen since we left the Ohio. Here, resting awhile, after making, as I supposed, various inquiries about their own families, Wawpawmawquaw related all the particulars of their late expedition, describing by the most significant gestures their ambush, our approach, their firing, the fall of one man and the escape of the other by swimming, their taking me prisoner, and finally exhibiting the scalp as a trophy of their exploit. This relation was heard by the hunters with profound attention, interrupted only at suitable times with proper expressions of wonder or of praise; after which, purchasing of them for a small silver brooch a few pieces of dried venison, we resumed our journey, traveling near the bank of the same stream (which I afterward found to be the Auglaize) until sunset, then supping on boiled venison, lay down to rest.

Still traveling down the Auglaize, about three hours after sunrise on the morning of the twelfth of July we came in sight of an Indian village, when Wawpawmawquaw, cutting a long pole, tied the scalp to the end of it and elevating it over his head raised the scalp-halloo, a shrill whoop, which both Indians repeated frequently until we entered the town. Here we found all its inhabitants assembled; more than fifty men, women, and children collected in front of the nearest cabin, who, as soon as the first salutations by the principal men were ended, seating themselves, some on logs and some on the ground, listened with deep attention while Wawpawmawquaw with that gravity of manner and those intonations of voice peculiar to Indian chiefs and warriors again told the story of my captivity. He was proceeding at last to describe the act of tomahawking and scalping the unfortunate white man when a little old Indian, suddenly springing upon me and throwing me down with violence, gave a loud shout, accompanied with many extravagant and furious gesticulations, and vociferating (as I was afterwards told) that he had vanquished his enemy. Immediately all the women began to scream and the children, down to the small papoose, setting up a long shrill war-whoop, gathered around me. I clung to Wawpawmaw-quaw, but young as I was I should have been compelled to run the gauntlet through the women and infant warriors had I not, from great debility occasioned by dysentery, been scarcely able to move faster than a walk.

About noon that day we arrived at another village on the Auglaize. Here, also, the inhabitants flocked out to meet us, and in like manner were entertained with an account of the late expedition of the Indians and the story of my captivity; but although the women and children manifested a great deal of curiosity, examining my dress and scanning me from head to feet, none of them offered me any rudeness. An elderly, noble-looking Indian, whom I took to be the village chief, now led us to his cabin, where his wife, who appeared to be a very mild and humane woman, gave us first some boiled hominy and then a little corn cake and boiled venison. This to me, at that time more than half starved, was a most delicious repast. I ate very heartily and rising from my seat and handing my kind hostess the bowl out of which I had eaten, bowing low, gratefully thanked her. She smiled and only said, "Onee, that is right, you are welcome," or, as if wishing to lessen the sense of the favor conferred, "It is nothing."

From this village we traveled leisurely on, occasionally passing an Indian hut, and toward evening stopped at the cabin of Wawpunnoo, a tall stout warrior, a brother of Wawpawmawquaw. His wife was quite a handsome woman, delicately formed and much fairer than the generality of squaws; she seemed to possess withal a very amiable disposition, and bore the churlish treatment of her husband with a meekness and patience that would adorn a Christian; although it was evident she felt mortified that others should witness his unkind conduct. By the by, the Indians in general are not kind and affectionate to their women, whom they treat rather as slaves than as companions, compelling them not only to perform the drudgery of the household, but even to work in the field, it being thought disgraceful for an Indian to labor. I have often seen families traveling, and while the poor squaw, bending under the weight of a heavy load, and the girls, carrying packs or the smaller children on their shoulders, were laboring along, the lazy Indian in front might be seen with nothing but his rifle and blanket, and the boys with only bow and arrows or a reed blowgun.

This night for the first time since my captivity I slept under a shelter; and lying on a deer skin with a blanket over me, slept comfortably. The next morning we breakfasted early and a little before noon of the thirteenth of July, after a journey of nearly six days and traveling about one hundred and eighty miles, we arrived at the point of the confluence of the Auglaize and Maumee, or Miami of the Lake. Here, disposing of their deer skins to a British Indian trader, the Indians crossed over the Miami to a small bark cabin near its bank and directly opposite to the point; and leaving me in charge of its occupant, an old widow, the mother of Wawpawmawquaw, departed for their homes, a village on the river about one mile below.

CHAPTER VI

COOH-COO-CHEEH, the old squaw in whose charge Wawpawmawquaw had left me, being in that advanced stage of life in which we seek for rest and quiet, apprehending no doubt from my squalid appearance and diseased state an increase of her cares and labors, at first received me with reluctance; but surveying my emaciated form and examining my scratched and festered limbs, my swelled feet, retaining when pressed the print of the finger, and my toes, from the friction of the sand collected in my moccasins in frequently fording creeks, raw and worn almost to the bone, her pity was excited, some of the dormant feelings of the mother were awakened, and she soon began to apply herself to my relief. Having first effected at the river a complete ablution of my person, she proceeded to wash my clothes, in the meantime compelling me to lie on a blanket for three or four hours under the scorching sun until my back was one entire blister; then boiling a strong decoction of red oak and wild cherry bark and dewberry root, of which I drank frequently, and in which I occasionally soaked my feet for several days, she effected in a short time a perfect cure.

She was a princess of the Wolf tribe of the Iroquois formerly living on the Sorel. Her person, about the ordinary stature, was stout and clumsy; her features were rather homely and her expression generally harsh and repulsive, though at times when her thoughts were withdrawn from the deep and weightier matters of futurity, or when, no longer conversing with the spirits of other worlds, she felt that she was an inhabitant of this and resumed her interest in its concerns, she was cheerful and occasionally quite sociable, relating many pleasant stories and amusing incidents of her early life. She was, besides, a sort of priestess to whom the Indians applied before going on any important war expedition, inquiring whether they should be successful; and from whom they generally received answers framed in such obscure and ambiguous terms as to confirm and increase her reputation, even when an expedition was most disastrous. Cooh-coo-cheeh was also esteemed a very great medicine woman, eminently skilful in the preparation of specifics believed to be of great efficacy, but whose extraordinary virtues were more particularly attributed to her powerful incantations and her influence with the good spirits, with whom she professed to hold daily intercourse.

Her husband had been a distinguished war chief of the Mohawks, a nation formerly occupying the country along the St. Lawrence as far as Lake Ontario and that bordering on Lakes George and Champlain. This nation toward the close of the seventeenth century, or about the year 1670, confederating with the Senecas, the Oneidas, the Cayugas, and the Onondagas, and forming what was then called the Five Nations (since, by the addition of the Tuscarawas expelled from North Carolina, called the Six Nations) conquering most of the nations southward and west of them, claimed the territory as far west as the Mississippi and southward to the Cherokee or Tennessee River. Utterly destroying some nations, of whom not a vestige now remains, and incorporating others whom they had vanquished, they formed a powerful confederacy, and besides, possessing superior bravery and consummate skill in war, they were formidable to the western tribes, in their wars with whom they were generally successful. The Mohawks were the early and firm allies of the British and maintained their supremacy over the northern tribes until about the year 1770, when, being totally defeated by the American colonists, they lost their ascendancy, yielded their claim of paramount authority, and, reduced and scattered, were in turn incorporated with other Indian nations over whom they had once ruled.

After this signal defeat and loss of the Mohawks the husband of Cooh-coo-cheeh with his family, consisting of his wife, three sons, and a daughter, had removed from the St. Lawrence and settled at the Shawnee village a mile below the mouth of the Auglaize. In the victory of the Indians over a part of the army of Harmar under Hardin and Wyllys, in October, 1790, in a furious charge made against the regulars, while in the act of tomahawking a soldier he received a mortal wound from a bayonet, and dying on his way home was buried on the bank of the Maumee about twenty miles from the battle-ground.[14]

---

[14]The "victory" by which Cooh-coo-cheeh was widowed was the second of Harmar's two battles with the Indians on the Maumee, October 22, 1790. The white force engaged

Soon after his death his widow chose her residence and erected her bark cabin on the spot now occupied by her; and having only a few months before, at the feast of the dead, with pious affection removed the remains of her late husband from their first resting place, interred them only a few rods above her dwelling, near to the war path, so that not only she might enjoy the happiness of conversing with him, but that his own spirit might be refreshed from viewing the warriors as they crossed the Maumee on their war expeditions, until having ended his probation and being prepared for his journey, he should travel to the final abode of good spirits in the land far west, abounding with game, and enjoy all those several delights which in the mind of an Indian constitute heaven. Buried in a sitting posture facing the west, by his side had been placed his rifle, tomahawk, knife, blanket, moccasins, and everything neces- sary for a hunter and a warrior; and his friends had, besides, thrown many little articles as presents into his grave, at the head of which they placed a post about four feet high, painted red and having near its top, rudely carved, the image of a face; while below was marked the number of scalps he had taken in battle, scalps of all colors, of hair of all lengths, which on some great occasions might be seen streaming in the wind, suspended from a high pole bending over his grave, where I once counted nineteen, torn from the heads of my unfortunate countrymen.

The family of Cooh-coo-cheeh consisted of a dark Indian girl (an orphan) two years my elder and a half Indian boy about a year younger than myself, both her grandchildren by her only daughter, now the wife of George Ironside, a British Indian trader living at the trading station

---

consisted of nearly 400 militia under Colonel Hardin and 60 regulars under Major Wyllys. When the encounter was joined the regulars fought valiantly, as usual, but the militia failed to support them and they were beaten off the field with the loss of many men, including Major Wyllys, their leader. Spencer's report of the way in which the Mohawk chief met death accords well with our knowledge from white sources of the conduct of the savages on this occasion. They seemed to have discarded their usual tactics of caution, and forced the fighting with the whites hand to hand. According to one narrator, "the militia they appeared to despise, and with all the undauntedness conceivable, threw down their guns and rushed upon the bayonets of the regular soldiers; a number of them fell, but being so far superior in numbers, the regulars were soon overpowered, for while the poor soldier had his bayonet in one Indian, two more would sink their tomahawks in his head." A letter written from Fort Harmar by Captain Jonathan Heart, six weeks after the battle of October 22, tells of a regular soldier who, "being surrounded and in the midst of the Indians, put his bayonet through six Indians, knocked down the seventh, and the soldier himself made the eighth dead man in the heap." The details of this exploit may be exaggerated, yet they serve to reflect the opinion of participants in the battle as to the extraordinary ardor with which the Indians pressed the attack.

on the high point directly opposite to her cabin, a few hundred yards above the mouth of the Auglaize.[15] The boy, reputed to be the son of the famous or rather infamous renegade, Simon Girty, was very sprightly, but withal passionate and wilful, a perfectly spoiled child, to whom his mother gave the Mohawk name of Ked-zaw-saw, while his grandmother called him Simo-ne; the girl, rather homely but cheerful and good natured, with bright, laughing eyes, was named So-tone-goo, but called by the old squaw, Quasay.

To those who have never seen the dwelling of an Indian priestess a description of the bark cabin of Cooh-coo-cheeh may perhaps be worth the reading. Covering an area of fourteen by twenty-eight feet, its frame was constructed of small poles, of which some, planted upright in the ground, served as posts and studs, supporting the ridge poles and eve bearers, while others firmly tied to these by thongs of hickory bark formed girders, braces, laths, and rafters. This frame was covered with large pieces of elm bark seven or eight feet long and three or four feet wide; which being pressed flat and well dried to prevent their curling, fastened to the poles by thongs of bark, formed the weather boarding and roof of the cabin. At its western end was a narrow doorway about six feet high, closed when necessary by a single piece of bark placed beside it, and fastened by a brace, set either within or on the outside as occasion required. Within, separated by a bark partition were two apartments, of which the inner one, seldom entered but by the old squaw, was occupied as a pantry, a spare bed room, and at times as a sanctuary, where she performed her incantations; the other, having on each side a low frame covered with bark and overspread with deerskins serving both for seats and bedsteads, was in common use by the family, both as a lodging, sitting, cooking, and eating room. On the ground in the center of this apartment was placed the fire; and over it, suspended from the ridge-pole in the middle of an aperture left for the passage of the smoke, was a wooden trammel for the convenience of cooking.

The site of this cabin was truly pleasant. It stood a few rods from the northern bank of the Maumee with its side fronting that river, on an elevated spot, from which the ground first gently descending about one

---

[15]George Ironside, at this time a leading trader of the Maumee Valley, was born in 1760 and died at Amherstburg, Canada, in 1830. For many years he served in the British Indian Department. He was a man of education, being an M.A. of King's College, Aberdeen. Of his humanity no further testimonial than Spencer's is needed. For numerous contemporary references to Ironside at this time, see "Henry Hay's Journal," edited by the present editor, in the Wisconsin Historical Society *Proceedings*, 1914, 208–61.

hundred yards northward thence gradually ascended to the top of the tableland bounding the narrow bottom, extending about two miles above and the same distance below. On the high ground was a beautiful open wood, principally of oak and hickory; while the bottom, with the exception of about five acres above the cabin cultivated with corn and a small spot around it, was covered with bushes, interspersed with saplings and a few blue and white ash and elm trees.

Both banks of the Maumee above the Auglaize were steep and high; that on which our cabin stood was covered with willows, while the opposite bank down to the point, being swept by the current, here slightly curving northeastwardly as it mingled with the waters of its tributary stream, was entirely bare. Immediately below the point the Auglaize, running from the southwest and bending northeastwardly near its mouth, washing the eastern side of the point, entering obliquely and mingling its current with the Maumee, occasioned in freshets a whirl and boiling of the water in the center, and strong eddies on both sides of the river; but in a low stage the water below the point and for some distance up each river was perfectly still. The Maumee, above the point about one hundred and twenty yards wide and directly below it a hundred and seventy, is here, in its center, in the lowest stage of water about seven feet deep; although its depth where it has a current is ordinarily not more than three. It abounds with excellent fish, which the Indians generally take with a gig or shoot with arrows and sometimes with rifle balls; but in this latter method of taking them, requiring great judgment and a practiced eye, they are rarely successful, particularly where the water is deep and very clear; the fish seeming to be within a few inches of the surface when he is at the same time so far below it that the ball, flattening, does not reach him.

On the south side of the Maumee for some distance below the mouth and extending more than a mile up the Auglaize to an Indian village, the low rich bottom, about three-quarters of a mile in width, was one entire field covered with corn, which, being in tassel, presented a beautiful appearance. It is, perhaps, not generally known that formerly the Indian women inhabiting large villages wherever it was practicable cultivated portions of the same field, separated from each other only by spaces of a few feet, and varying in size according to the number and strength of their families; seldom raising corn as an article of commerce, but merely to furnish bread for their own subsistence. Around these large fields they made no inclosures; nor, indeed, having no cattle, hogs, nor sheep, were fences necessary. As for their few horses, they were either driven out into the woods or secured near their cabins, and having bells on, were easily prevented from trespassing by the boys, whose duty it was, by turns, while amusing themselves with their bows and arrows, to protect the fields.

I had lived in my new habitation about a week; and having given up all hope of escaping, which I now considered impossible, began to regard it as my future home. True, the home from which I had been torn and the beloved parents from whom I felt that I was forever separated were seldom from my thoughts; yet I strove to be cheerful, and by my ready obedience to ingratiate myself with Cooh-coo-cheeh, for whose kindness I felt grateful; and who, with the blessing of Divine Providence, having restored me to health, took some pains to comfort and amuse me. Her son-in-law, a respectable Indian trader, supplied her occasionally with a few necessaries; while from the Indians, who consulted her on most important matters, she received presents of venison and skins and brooches, the common circulating medium among them. Her household furniture consisted of a large brass kettle for washing and sugar making; a deep, close-covered, copper hominy kettle; a few knives, tin cups, pewter and horn spoons, sieves, wooden bowls, and baskets of various sizes; a hominy block, and four beds and bedding comprising each a few deerskins and two blankets; so that, altogether, her circumstances were considered quite comfortable.

Her dress like that of the old squaws in general was very plain and simple, consisting of a calico shirt extending about six inches below the waist and fastened at the bosom with a silver brooch; a stroud or petticoat, simply a yard and a half of six quarter blue cloth with white selvedge, wrapped around her waist and confined with a girdle, and extending a little below the knee; a pair of leggings or Indian stockings of the same cloth, sewed so as to fit the leg, leaving a border of two inches projecting from the outside and extending to the instep, and a pair of plain moccasins. The form of the dress is the same among the Indian women of all ranks and ages, varying only in its quality and in the richness and variety with which it is adorned; its ornaments not being regulated by rank or station, but by the ability of the wearer. All the young and middle-aged among the women are passionately fond of finery, the young belles, particularly, having the tops of their moccasins curiously wrought with beads, ribbons, and porcupine quills; the borders of their leggings and the bottom and edges of their strouds tastily bound with ribbons, edged with beads of various colors; and frequently on their moccasins and leggings small tufts of deer's hair, dyed red and confined in small pieces of tin, rattling as they walked and forcibly reminding one of the "tinkling ornaments" worn by the Jewish women.

Besides these ornaments, according to their ability they covered the bosom, shoulders, sides, and bottoms of their shirts (sometimes made of cross-barred silk handkerchiefs) with large and small silver brooches, and wore on their wrists and arms silver bracelets from one to four inches in width.

Nor is the fondness for show confined to the women; on the contrary it is even stronger in the men, who in addition to the ornaments worn by the women wear large silver medals and gorgets on the breast, silver rings in the nose, and heavy pieces of silver in the ears, the rims of which, being separated from the cartilage by cutting, are weighed down two or three inches from the head. A trifling circumstance, which I omitted to mention, may illustrate their extreme love of show. When captured my roundabout and pantaloons were of plain summer wear, with covered mould buttons; but my vest was of blue silk, double breasted, with two rows of small plated sugarloaf buttons, which, attracting their attention, the Indians had several times examined, supposing them to be silver. On the second night after leaving the Ohio, the companion of Wawpawmawquaw, taking my vest, cut off both rows of buttons including a strip of two inches of the silk on each side, and carefully folding them up put them in his bullet pouch. Surprised at his conduct and unable to form any idea of his motive in spoiling my vest, I thought he was actuated by a savage malignity merely, and felt not a little chagrined and indignant when, just before entering the first Indian village, I saw him fasten the spoils of my vest around his legs as garters, contrasting strangely with his greasy leathern leggings.

It was now about the twenty-first of July, and being a leisure time with Cooh-coo-cheeh, principally, perhaps, to indulge her own inclination, and partly to amuse me, she took me on a visit to the Shawnee village below us. We were kindly received by Wawpawmawquaw, whose wife, a very pleasant and rather pretty woman of twenty-five, according to custom set before us some refreshment consisting of some dried green corn boiled with beans and dried pumpkins, and making, as I thought, a very excellent dish.

After spending a few hours with this family we went to pay our respects to the village chief, the celebrated Blue Jacket.[16] This chief was

---

[16]Blue Jacket's village was on the Auglaize River, a mile above its junction with the Maumee. This Shawnee chief was one of the most active leaders of the red race in its conflict with the whites for the possession of the Old Northwest. He was one of the leaders of the Indians in St. Clair's defeat, and is supposed to have been their principal leader against Wayne's army at Fallen Timbers. After this defeat of the Indians, Blue Jacket yielded and was one of the signers of the Treaty of Greenville. Blue Jacket is a good example of the better type of Indian chieftains.

the most noble in appearance of any Indian I ever saw. His person, about six feet high, was finely proportioned, stout, and muscular; his eyes large, bright, and piercing; his forehead high and broad; his nose aquiline; his mouth rather wide, and his countenance open and intelligent, expressive of firmness and decision; he was considered one of the most brave and accomplished of the Indian chiefs, second only to Little Turtle[17] and Buck-on-ge-ha-la,[18] having signalized himself on many occasions, particularly in the defeats of Colonel Hardin and General St. Clair. He held (as I was told) the commission and received the half pay of a brigadier general from the British crown. On this day, receiving a visit from The Snake, chief of a neighboring Shawnee village, and from Simon Girty, he was dressed in a scarlet frock coat, richly laced with gold and confined around his waist with a party-colored sash, and in red leggings and moccasins ornamented in the highest style of Indian fashion. On his shoulders he wore a pair of gold epaulets, and on his arms broad silver bracelets; while from his neck hung a massive silver gorget and a large medallion of His Majesty, George III. Around his lodge were hung rifles, war clubs, bows and arrows, and other implements of war; while the skins of deer, bear, panther, and otter, the spoils of the chase, furnished pouches for tobacco, or mats for seats and beds. His wife was a remarkably fine looking woman; his daughters, much fairer than the generality of Indian women, were quite handsome; and his two sons, about eighteen and twenty years old, educated by the British, were very intelligent.

One of the visitors of Blue Jacket (The Snake) was a plain, grave chief of sage appearance; the other, Simon Girty, whether it was from prejudice, associating with his look the fact that he was a renegade, the murderer of his own countrymen, racking his diabolic invention to

---

[17]Little Turtle was born on Eel River in 1752 and died at Fort Wayne in 1812. He was an inveterate foe of the Americans until the Treaty of Greenville, in which he bore a prominent part as spokesman for his race. Convinced of the hopelessness of further resistance to the whites, he pledged a religious observance of the treaty, and until his death this pledge was faithfully kept. Little Turtle's greatest military exploit was the destruction of St. Clair's army in 1791.

[18]Buckhongelas was head chief of the Delawares. He was an active leader in the warfare of 1790–95, but acquiesced in the results of Wayne's victory over his race and thereafter counseled his followers to preserve friendship with the Americans. In his *Tales and Sketches from the Queen City* (Cincinnati, 1838), Benjamin Drake tells several interesting stories about Buckhongelas. Among others he relates that at the Treaty of Fort McIntosh of 1785 Buckhongelas was present with other chiefs. The American commissioners were George Rogers Clark, Arthur Lee, and Richard Butler. After the peace chiefs had made their speeches the war chief of the Delawares, Buckhongelas, rose and passing by Butler and Lee without noticing them took General Clark by the hand and said: "I thank the Great Spirit for having this day brought together two such great warriors as Buckhongelas and General Clark."

inflict new and more excruciating tortures, or not; his dark shaggy hair, his low forehead; his brows contracted and meeting above his short flat nose; his gray sunken eyes, averting the ingenuous gaze; his lips thin and compressed, and the dark and sinister expression of his countenance, to me seemed the very picture of a villain. He wore the Indian costume, but without any ornament; and his silk handkerchief, while it supplied the place of a hat, hid an unsightly wound in his forehead. On each side, in his belt, was stuck a silver-mounted pistol, and at his left hung a short broad dirk, serving occasionally the uses of a knife. He made of me many inquiries; some about my family and the particulars of my captivity; but more of the strength of the different garrisons, the number of American troops at Fort Washington, and whether the President intended soon to send another army against the Indians. He spoke of the wrongs he had received at the hands of his countrymen, and with fiendish exultation of the revenge he had taken. He boasted of his exploits, of the number of his victories, and of his personal prowess; then, raising his handkerchief and exhibiting the deep wound in his forehead (which I was afterwards told was inflicted by the tomahawk of the celebrated Indian chief, Brant, in a drunken frolic) said it was a saber cut which he received in battle at St. Clair's defeat; adding with an oath that he had "sent the damned Yankee officer" that gave it "to hell." He ended by telling me that I would never see home; but if I should "turn out to be a good hunter and a brave warrior I might one day be a chief." His presence and conversation having rendered my situation painful, I was not a little relieved when a few hours after, ending our visit, we returned to our quiet lodge on the bank of the Maumee.

CHAPTER VII

A FEW DAYS after my visit to Blue Jacket's village I accompanied Cooh-coo-cheeh over to the point, the residence of her daughter. On this high ground (since the site of Fort Defiance, erected by General Wayne in 1794) extending from the Maumee a quarter of a mile up the Auglaize, about two hundred yards in width, was an open space, on the west and south of which were oak woods with hazel undergrowth. Within this opening, a few hundred yards above the point on the steep high bank of the Auglaize were five or six cabins and log houses, inhabited principally by Indian traders. The most northerly, a large hewed log house divided below into three apartments, was occupied as a warehouse, store, and dwelling by George Ironside, the most wealthy and influential of the traders on the point. Next to his were the houses of Pirault (Pero), a French baker, and M'Kenzie, a Scot, who in addition to merchandising followed the occupation of a silversmith, exchanging with the Indians his brooches, eardrops, and other silver ornaments at an enormous profit for skins and furs.[19] Still farther up were several other families of French and English; and two American prisoners, Henry Ball, a soldier taken at St. Clair's defeat, and his wife, Polly Meadows, captured at the same time, were allowed to live here and by labor to pay their masters the price of their ransom; he by boating to the rapids of the Maumee, and she by washing and sewing. Fronting the house of Ironside, and about fifty yards from the bank, was a small

---

[19] This was John Kinzie, who in 1804 settled at Chicago and has since come to be popularly known as the "father" of the inland metropolis. Two years before this Kinzie was located at Miamitown (modern Fort Wayne). "Henry Hay's Journal," already referred to, contains much concerning Kinzie's doings and manner of life at this time. An account of Kinzie's career is given in the present editor's *Chicago and the Old Northwest*, 145–52.

stockade enclosing two hewed log houses, one of which was occupied by James Girty[20] (brother of Simon), the other, occasionally, by McKee and Elliott, British Indian agents living at Detroit.

From this station I had a fine view of the large village more than a mile south on the east side of the Auglaize, of Blue Jacket's town, and of the Maumee River for several miles below, and of the extensive prairie covered with corn directly opposite, and forming together a very pleasant landscape.[21] I spent this day very pleasantly among the traders, dining with Mr. Ironside, who treated me with great kindness. I found him to be a very sociable and intelligent man, humane and benevolent. He seemed much interested in the story of my captivity, appeared to sympathize with me, gave me some useful advice and direction for the regulation of my conduct, and a great deal of information relative to the Indians, their history, customs, and manners.

On the following day I was highly gratified in seeing at our cabin my late townsman, William Moore, who had just returned from a trip to the Rapids about sixty miles below. Moore was a stout, sinewy, muscular man, six feet two inches high; active, bold, and daring; combining the qualities and peculiarities of the western boatman and hunter; one who in Kentucky would in former years have been termed "half horse, half alligator"; a practiced marksman, who at fifty steps, with his rifle, "off hand," often "drove the center" and seldom failed to "cut the black": on the keel pushing the first pole, and in running, jumping, wrestling, and other athletic exercises having few superiors. Fearless and lawless, he was governed only by his own sense of propriety and right, naturally good humored and obliging, but when roused a perfect savage; and bold and powerful must have been the man that would encounter and overcome him.

He had been taken prisoner by Wawpawmawquaw, his brother Cawta-maw-waw-quaw (Black Loon) and three other Indians a few months

---

[20]As already noted, James Girty had assisted the British against his native land during the Revolution. At its close he established a trading house at St. Mary's on the Maumee, at a place later known as Girty's Town. After Harmar's attack in 1790 Girty withdrew to the Auglaize, from which he again retreated before Wayne's attack of 1794 to Detroit, and, later, to Canada. There he died April 5, 1817.

[21]The junction of the Auglaize with the Maumee was, like the modern site of Fort Wayne, one of the leading centers of Indian activity in the northwest. When Wayne's army advanced to the Maumee in the summer of 1794 the leader hoped to deliver a telling blow against the Indians at this point. The timely warning of a deserter enabled the red men to flee in advance of Wayne's arrival; but their villages, extending for several miles along the river, with cornfields more extensive than Wayne had ever seen before "from Canada to Florida," were razed by him; while, on the site of the British traders' settlement at the junction of the rivers, Fort Defiance was reared. From this fort the modern city of Defiance, on the same site, takes its name.

preceding my captivity, about five miles north of Columbia on the waters of Mill Creek, where he had been hunting. He had just killed a fine doe, and having lashed it on his shoulders had proceeded a few steps on his return home when the Indians, who had been watching his movements and waiting until he should be encumbered with his load, fired upon him from his right. One of their balls grazed his right shoulder blade, another passing through the carpus, or compact bones of the wrist, rendered powerless his left hand. Springing forward on the instant, for the first hundred yards even with his load he outran the Indians; meanwhile, placing his rifle on his left shoulder and throwing his wounded hand over it, with his right cutting the lashings, he disencumbered himself of his burden and in a few minutes distanced all but two of his pursuers. Gaining the top of the ridge and looking back upon the Indians, the foremost of whom were several rods behind him, he gave a loud whoop, and deridingly slapping his thigh bounded off like a deer to the foot of the hill. Here, failing in the attempt to leap a creek, his feet slipped on the edge of the opposite bank and he fell backward into the water. By the time he had risen to his feet and recovered his rifle, which had fallen into the water, he was overtaken by Wawpaw-mawquaw, who, leaping down the bank, twice snapped his pistol at him. Moore, meantime, leveling his rifle, also twice attempted to shoot the Indian; but unfortunately its priming was wet, and he had no opportunity to renew it. Clubbing his gun he next attempted to strike down his adversary, but his left hand being powerless his stroke was easily parried. He now threw down his rifle and drawing his knife was just about to close in deadly strife when the brother of Wawpawmaw-quaw that moment reaching the spot, interfered. Becoming faint from the loss of blood, seeing the remaining Indians close at hand, and considering further resistance or attempt to escape useless, Moore picked up his rifle and surrendered it to Wawpawmawquaw, who, extending to him his hand, received him as his prisoner.

On his arrival at Blue Jacket's village, Moore, being only a private prisoner to one whose family had no manes to appease or blood to retribute, was not subjected to the disposal of a council; but custom immemorial requiring that as a man and a warrior he should run the gauntlet, an early hour was fixed for the interesting exhibition. That day soon arrived; and men, women, and children, invited from the neighboring villages, flocked to the capital of the Shawnees, anticipating as much pleasure as we would expect at the celebration of our nation's anniversary. Here, after gratifying their curiosity in examining the prisoner, armed with clubs, switches, and other instruments of punishment they arranged themselves facing each other in two rows about seven feet apart and numbering more than two hundred persons, each distant four or five feet from each other, extending three hundred yards along the level space between the village and the Maumee River. The chiefs and principal warriors stood at the head of the lines within a few rods of the cabin selected as the goal, while the rest of the men with the women and the youths, promiscuously occupied the other parts.

Moore was now led out and stripped to the waist, when the Indians, aware of his strength and activity, tied together his wrists, for the double purpose of hindering his speed and preventing him from retaliating on his tormentors, yet so as to afford him the means of protecting his face. Starting a short distance from the head of the lines, he soon bounded through them; and breathing a few moments, returning with the same speed, had reached the middle of his course when the Indians, fearing that from his fleetness he would run through with little injury (as most of their blows instead of falling on his back fell clattering on each others' sticks) half closing their ranks attempted to obstruct his progress. Appealing in vain to their sense of honor and justice, frequently crying (as he told me) "Honor bright!" and "Fair play!" and finding that he would probably be severely beaten, he undertook himself to redress his wrongs; and so effectually did he use his feet, head, and right wrist, kicking some, striking down others, and with his head overturning a number, that the rest readily made way, and opening for him an ample passage, amidst the shouts of the warriors he soon reached the goal. Having passed the ordinary trial he was now congratulated as a brave man and by some applauded for his late resistance, all but the sufferers being highly diverted at his successful expedient to rid himself of a severe beating.

Moore was a great favorite of Cooh-coo-cheeh, to whose comfort and accommodation he had largely contributed. But a short time before my arrival he had added to her solitary room an additional cabin, and now, preparatory to the feast of green corn, he was engaged in erecting for her a bark shed, closed at the back and facing our cabin, a few rods distant on the west, and elevated about three feet from the ground for the accommodation of her more aged guests, who, unable to take any active part in them, might here witness the exercises and sports of the day.

It was on a pleasant morning about the middle of August, when the ears of corn, grown to full size, were yet in the soft milky state in which they are used for roasting, that the three sons of Cooh-coo-cheeh, with their wives; her daughter, with her husband, Mr. Ironside; Captain Walker and some other Shawnee warriors with their wives, and a few old squaws, in compliance with her invitation assembled at our cabin to celebrate the feast of green corn. This is a festival said to be similar to that of "first fruits" among the Jews (and by some used as an argument to prove that the aborigines of America were descendants of that nation), when the more wealthy and influential among the Indians of the same tribe, ostensibly to evidence their gratitude to the Great Spirit for his manifold mercies, inviting the members and relatives of their respective families, feast them principally on green corn variously cooked and entertain them with different games and sports; usually crowning their festivities with copious draughts of "fire water"—either rum or whiskey.

Here, after the usual salutations at meeting, when all were gathered and seated on the grass and the pipe according to custom had several times passed around the circle, a venerable Indian arose and with much solemnity of tone and earnestness of manner addressed them. He spoke (as Mr. Ironside afterward informed me) of the distinguishing favor of the Great Spirit to his red children, the first and most honorable of the human race, to whom he had given the vast country stretching from the sun's rising place in the far east to where it sets in the great waters beyond the Rocky Mountains; extending from the frozen sea of the north to the boundless salt waters of the south; yielding abundantly corn for bread, supplying meat and clothing for their families from the buffalo, the elk, the deer, and every variety of wild game with which the forest once abounded; producing spontaneously the most valuable medicinal plants, furnishing specifics for every disease to which his red children were exposed; of their obligations to him for all these benefits, especially for sending them fruitful showers and now blessing them with an earnest of a good crop of corn, and that they ought to evidence their sense of obligation to Him by gratefully feasting on His bounties there provided for them and by heartily engaging in the manly sports and exercises of the day.

He then spoke of the "palefaces," whom he represented as the first murderers and oppressors; ascribed their own sad reverses to the anger of the Great Spirit for affording these murderers an asylum on their shores; of their duty to exterminate if possible these intruders on their soil, at least to drive them south of the Ohio. He said that their late victories over the whites, particularly their signal defeat of St. Clair, were evidences of the returning favor of the Great Spirit; and concluded by exhorting them to deeds of valor and to conquest of their natural enemies as a certain passport to the boundless hunting grounds in the far, far west, "beyond the vast waters," where the Great Spirit would never "suffer the palefaces" to enter. This speech was listened to by all with deep attention, the auditors improving each deep pause to utter some monosyllable expressive of the various feelings that by turns inspired them; but at the concluding sentence, as if actuated by one sentiment, simultaneously springing to their feet and uttering a shrill and prolonged whoop, with great animation they commenced their sports.

The first of these was running on foot over a straight course of about one hundred yards, in which the principal competitors were the White and Black Loons, Wawpunnoo, and Captain Walker; Moore not being allowed at the beginning to join in their sports. And here for the first time having an opportunity of witnessing the fleetness of the Indians, I noticed that in running as in walking they turned their toes in, hindering the full force of the muscles of the leg; and that their movements resembled more the bounding of the deer than the more rapid steps of the whites, whose lower, forward efforts bore them only onward. And I am satisfied that, although from habit continuing to breathe freely, the Indians may run longer at great speed, yet in a short race they are generally less fleet than the whites. Wawpawmawquaw, whose movements were lower and more rapid, won the race; though Moore swore that he could give him twenty steps and beat him in a hundred yards.

In the wrestling that followed Wawpunnoo (brother of the Loons) and Captain Walker, both tall and powerful men, bore off the palm; but in repeated trials with each other, with various success, Walker was acknowledged victor. Wawpawmawquaw, however, having been several times severely thrown by Walker, now insisted that he should wrestle with Moore. To this Walker objected, intimating that it would be rather a stoop to wrestle with a prisoner; but the Loon insisting and at the same time leading Moore forward, he reluctantly advanced to meet him. Their first essays as is usual with practiced wrestlers were but partial trials of each other's strength and skill; but at length exerting their powers, the contest was long and apparently doubtful; each by turns being raised from his feet, seemed about to be thrown with violence by his antagonist or bent to the ground by his powerful arms when Moore, availing himself of an unguarded movement of his adversary, with a trip of his foot and a sudden twist of his body threw him to the ground, yet partially with his arms sustaining him while falling, so that he suffered no injury. Mortified at his failure and more than half angry, Walker sprung to his feet, and again closing with Moore, straining every muscle of his body, put forth all his strength. The struggle, however, was short; for Moore being now excited, losing sight of his former prudence, by a powerful effort raising his antagonist on his hip pitched him heels over head, stretching with violence his whole length upon the ground. This occasioned a loud "Waugh!" from the other Indians and no small gratification to the White Loon; but Moore, perceiving that he had roused the resentment of Walker and excited the jealousy of the rest, strove to allay their feelings, and by magnifying the strength of his antagonist and ascribing his own success rather to accident than to superior power and skill, soon succeeded in restoring good humor.

It being now about noon, the Indians suspended their sports to partake of the splendid feast provided by Cooh-coo-cheeh, consisting of boiled jerk and fish, stewed squirrels and venison, and green corn boiled some in the ear and some cut from the cob and mixed with beans, besides squashes and roasted pumpkins. For bread, besides that prepared in the ordinary way from corn meal we had some made of the green corn cut from the cob and pounded in a mortar until it was brought to the consistency of thick cream, then being salted and poured into a sort of mould of an oblong form more than half the length and twice the thickness of a man's hand, made of corn leaves, and baked in the ashes, was very palatable. The guests did ample justice to the entertainment, eating very heartily out of the wooden bowls in which their dinner was served and which they held in their laps, using their own knives to cut their meat, which they held in their fingers, and the horn, wooden, and pewter spoons of their hostess in eating their succotash; each man and woman as they finished their dinner setting down their bowl saying, "Ooway, nelah, netape hooloo"; literally, "I have done; my stomach is full." Having all dined and enjoyed for a few minutes the (with them) great luxury of smoking, a small keg of rum was produced, to the great gratification of the guests, all of whom, both men and women, took a hearty draught; when the men, giving their knives and tomahawks in charge to Cooh-coo-cheeh, arose to renew their sports.

CHAPTER VIII

THE INDIANS ARE extravagantly fond of spirituous liquor; not only the men, but the women, when they can obtain it, drinking to excess. Aware, however, of its mischievous consequences, they always before deliberately commencing a drunken revel select some one to remain sober, to whose charge they commit their knives, tomahawks, and other dangerous weapons, and whose duty it is carefully to secrete and retain these until after their carousal, when they shall have become perfectly sober; so that very rarely at their revels more serious injuries occur than bruised eyes or bloody noses. And when at their drunken bouts brawls take place and blows and wounds succeed, the injuries they suffer are entirely overlooked when sober; all their acts committed in a state of ebriety being ascribed wholly to the "fire water."

On their way home (usually at night) from their carousals, they always give notice of their coming, singing or rather roaring their drunken song, "Ha yaw ki-you-wan-nie, Hi haw nit-ta-koo-pee," the notes of which, rather plaintive and dirge-like, are more varied than their generally monotonous tunes; and sung quicker or slower, louder or less vociferously, not only indicate the age and temper, but mark with great certainty the degree of intoxication of the individual; one very drunk prolonging each note, sometimes sounding as if the singer had made a sudden lurch to one side or a stagger on the other. If the Indian be one whom drunkenness renders more savage and brutal, his wife or any member of his family with whom he may have been offended when sober now has a warning, which is seldom neglected, to keep out of his way; as he not infrequently avails himself of the cover of ebriety to revenge with impunity some injury he had received when sober.

At such times and under such circumstances it is peculiarly danger-ous for prisoners (many of whom fall a sacrifice to the brutal barbarity of drunken Indians) to encounter them. Once when in company with

White Loon and Moore, who were shooting fish near Blue Jacket's village, I saw from the canoe the body of a youth of fourteen (who with his sister, a girl of sixteen, had been taken prisoners by the Indians from some settlement on the Ohio a short time after my captivity) who had been tomahawked and scalped and mangled in the most brutal manner by his drunken master, who, not taking the trouble even to bury him, left him to rot near the edge of the Maumee. I myself have often been obliged in the middle of winter, when the ground was covered with a deep snow, at the well-known, dreaded sounds "ki-you-wan-nie," to spring from my bed and seizing only a blanket, run and hide behind the nearest log or tree or throw myself down in the snow, where I have laid for more than an hour, not daring to move until the drunkard had gone off, and once I narrowly escaped death.

I had, unfortunately, offended Black Loon, who some nights afterward, returning home drunk from the Miami village a few miles west of us, came so near to our cabin before I was aware of his approach that I had scarcely time to escape. Entering the door he inquired for me, and being told that I was absent struck his knife several times through the skins on my bunk; then seizing a cat which lay near him, threw it on the fire and placing his foot upon it kept it there (the poor animal squalling most piteously the while) until Cooh-coo-cheeh, jerking it out, threw it into the snow. This poor Indian, fighting in our cause in the late war with Great Britain, was unfortunately killed near Manary's blockhouse a few miles from Bellefontaine by one of our rangers, supposing him to be a spy of the enemy.

At the close of the last chapter I left the Indians, who had just dined, about to resume their festive games; and as it may possibly interest some of my readers I will briefly describe one or two more, ending the sports of the feast of green corn.

The men now formed a circle, within and near the edge of which one of the strongest, lying on his back, held firmly in his hands between his raised knees a piece of rawhide, made soft by soaking and so slippery from greasing as to require a powerful grasp and a strong hand to wrest it from his grip. Following each other at the distance of about three feet, and moving several times around the circle in quick time, with elastic step, sinking alternately on each foot, and singing, "A yaw whano hiegh, how-wa-yow-wa" in one of their most monotonous tunes, each Indian in succession, giving a loud "whoop-haw," suddenly stooped and firmly grasping the rawhide strove to draw it from the hands of its holder. Failing in this, or drawing it suddenly from his hands, some not infrequently measured their length upon the ground to the no small amusement of the others; but the wresting it from the hands of the holder or raising him by it from the ground erect upon his feet was held to be a proof of superior strength.

Dancing now began, the men moving in an outer and the women in an inner circle, stepping lightly, and rather gracefully sinking with a rocking motion, first on one foot, then on the other; or changing the form, facing each other in lines, sometimes springing up briskly with a sort of galloping motion, at others, with their bodies bent forward slowly raising both feet at once and bringing them down heavily, uttering a "hiegh" at every jump, while an old man, pounding with one stick upon a small drum, sang at the same time slowly or more lively according to the kind of dance, regulating the steps of the dancers, who kept exact time with the music.

It was now the middle of the afternoon and both men and women with the exception of Cooh-coo-cheeh were more than half drunk. Moore had prudently retired with Mr. Ironside across the Maumee, and I had withdrawn to the corn fields; where, however, looking through a small hole in the back of the shed I could without danger witness the movements of the Indians. They now drank more frequently; some dancing singly, others in groups; some singing, some whooping; and some quarreling, until at length "uproar wild and deep confusion reigned." About this time Wawpawmawquaw, smarting, probably, under the recollection of the severe falls he had received from Walker, laying hold of him and insisting on another trial of his skill in wrestling, being unfortunately thrown into the fire and severely burned, served as a signal for bringing the festivities to a close; and in a very short time, staggering off in different directions, all departed to their respective homes.

Little worth relating occurred for nearly two months. In the meantime, having nothing to do except to bring water and collect wood for cooking, I had some leisure which I occupied in hunting with a bow and arrow, in the use of which I became quite expert, frequently shooting birds and at one time killing a fine rabbit, which I bore to the cabin with no small degree of pride and to the great satisfaction of the old squaw, to whom it furnished a delicious repast, and of Sotonegoo, who congratulated me, telling me that I would soon become a man and a hunter. Sometimes, too, I was permitted to visit the trader's station on the point, where I was always welcomed by Mr. Ironside and treated with great kindness by his wife, the daughter of Cooh-coo-cheeh.

It was on one of these visits in the woods above the point, as I before related, that I saw Wells, then a prisoner at large among the Indians, who, having learned my name, inquired very particularly about my family, their residence and rank. The information which I gave him he soon communicated to the officer commanding at Post Vincennes, by whom it was sent to Colonel Wilkinson[22] at Fort Washington and by him immediately to my father. Through the influence of General Washington letters were obtained from the British minister at Philadelphia to Colonel Simcoe, governor of Upper Canada,[23] and an agent was dispatched by my friends through the state of New York to Niagara; so that, while abandoning all hope of seeing again my home and my beloved kindred, I was striving to become reconciled to my fate, active preparations were making for my release and measures were in operation which, under the blessing of Providence, in a few months afterward resulted in my deliverance.

About the middle of October the Indians, learning through their spies that either an expedition against some of their towns was contemplated by the Americans or that provisions were on their way to supply the outposts under a strong convoy, soon assembled a force of two hundred warriors (Shawnees and Miamies) under the celebrated Little Turtle and marched to attack them.[24] On their way to join the Miamies, who had encamped near the point, the two Loons and about fifty Shawnee warriors from Snake's town and Blue Jacket's village halted near our cabin and sent to consult Cooh-coo-cheeh about the success of their expedition. The old woman immediately entered her sanctuary, where she remained nearly an hour, during a part of which time, sitting under the shed, I could hear the noise as of a stick striking the sides of the cabin and the beds and particularly the kettles within it; and afterward a low humming sound of the voice, at which time I supposed she was uttering her incantations. Coming out soon after with a countenance unusually animated, though with a look of great wildness, she stretched out both arms and then gradually bringing the tips of her fingers together as if encircling something exclaimed, "Mechee! mechee! mechee!" which the Indians, instantly interpreting to be "Many scalps,

---

[22]This was James Wilkinson, who later became major-general of the United States army. Although one of the leading men of his time, his dealings with Aaron Burr and with the Spanish government have left a cloud upon his reputation with posterity.

[23]Governor John Graves Simcoe was a native of England and had been educated at Eton and Oxford. He entered the British army in 1771 and served through the American Revolution, being a member of the army surrendered by Cornwallis at Yorktown. He entered parliament in 1790, but the next year was appointed lieutenant-governor of Upper Canada, which position he filled during the four years, 1792–96. He was then sent to San Domingo, from which place at the end of two years he returned to England, where he died in 1806.

[24]This account relates to the assault by the Indians upon the troops of Major Adair near Fort St. Clair, November 9, 1792. Six soldiers were killed and five wounded, and a large number of pack horses driven off by the Indians.

many prisoners, and much plunder," reported to the party, who, flushed with the confident expectation of success, immediately proceeded to join the main body.

I had never before seen so large a force of Indian warriors, and while I could not but admire their fine forms and warlike appearance as they marched in single file to the river or stood erect in their canoes, with their rifles in their hands, crossing the Maumee, I shuddered at the thought of the lives that would be taken and the hundreds that through their instrumentality would soon be made widows, orphans, and childless. Young as I then was I could not help at times looking on the old woman with superstitious fear, mingled with awe. I did not believe that she was divinely inspired, but thought it more than probable that she held intercourse with evil spirits; nor was that fear and awe lessened when about the middle of November the Indians under Little Turtle returned victorious, having defeated a body of troops, principally Kentuckians (or Semonthe, as they termed them) near Fort St. Clair, taking several scalps, a large number of horses, and a great deal of baggage. Wawpawmawquaw and his brother had each a good horse and a number of new blankets; and some of the Indians packed home tents, camp kettles, and many other articles. The Shawnees gave Cooh-coo-cheeh six blankets and several pounds of tobacco, besides a small keg of whiskey (part of their spoils) in gratitude for the aid which they doubted not she had afforded them in achieving their victory; while their late success, if possible, increased their confidence in her supposed supernatural power.

The weather had now become cold and my summer clothes, being not only too thin for the season but nearly worn out, were thrown aside; and a white shirt, blanket capote, blue leggings, and waist cloth supplied their place, so that I was dressed in full Indian costume.

Although the labor of gathering their corn was over I found pretty constant employment; I had now to make fires, carry water both for cooking and drinking, wash the hominy when boiled in ashes, and assist the old woman in getting wood. One afternoon in December Cooh-coo-cheeh, being engaged, sent me alone to cut and bring home an armful of wood. Taking the axe, the pecawn (a long strap for tying up the wood) and our faithful dog, who generally accompanied me, I went about a quarter of a mile up the bottom; where, having cut some wood and tied it into a bundle, I was just about to place it on my back when the dog, moving off cautiously a few rods, sat down near a small tree, where growling fiercely and striking the ground with his tail he first looked up toward the top of a sapling and then at me, as if to inform me there was game there and to ask my assistance. Picking up the axe I walked deliberately to the dog and following the direction of his eyes saw on a limb about sixteen feet from the ground an animal of a dark gray color mixed with red, with a white belly and round head, altogether resembling a cat, but four times larger than the largest tame cat, and crouched like that animal when ready to spring upon its prey. Ignorant of its nature and unapprehensive of danger I threw several sticks at it to induce it to come down; at length, hitting it severely on the head, it sprang to the ground within a few feet of me when the dog, instantly seizing it, a fierce contest ensued. The dog, being strong, active, and courageous, several times caught the animal by the throat, but was as often compelled to let go his hold, so fiercely and powerfully did his antagonist, drawing up his hind feet, apply his sharp claws to his breast and sides. Indeed, I now began to fear he would conquer the dog, whose ardor seemed to have considerably abated and who fought with greater caution; approaching with the axe and taking advantage of an opportunity when the dog again attempted to seize the throat of the animal, I was so fortunate as to hit him a severe blow on the head, completely stunning him; then left him to his enraged antagonist, who soon finished the work of death. The dog, though severely wounded, appeared to be delighted; now standing over his fallen enemy as if exulting in his death and now jumping around me, wagging his tail with pleasure. For myself, I turned the animal over several times; marked his length, which from his nose to the end of his tail I judged to be about four feet; then examining him particularly, for the first time suspected that he was either a wild cat or a young panther.

Leaving my wood and shouldering my prize I marched home, and with no small exultation threw my load down before Cooh-coo-cheeh, who, raising her hands with surprise, exclaimed, "Waugh haugh-h! Pooshun!" It proved, indeed, to be a large male wild cat; an animal equally insidious and dangerous, according to its size and strength, as a panther; and which, but for the presence of the dog and my ignorance of its nature and of my danger, might have destroyed me. This exploit, with which the old woman associated great courage and daring, raised me very much in her estimation. She heard all the particulars of the affair with great satisfaction, and frequently saying, "Enee, wessah" (that is right, that is good), said I would one day become a great hunter, and placing her forefingers together (by which sign the Indians represent marriage) and then pointing to Sotonegoo, told me that when I should become a man I should have her for a wife.

I had now acquired a sufficient knowledge of the Shawnee tongue to understand all ordinary conversation and, indeed, the greater part of all that I heard (accompanied, as their conversation and speeches were, with the most significant gestures); and often in the long winter evenings listened with much pleasure and sometimes with deep interest to Cooh-coo-cheeh, as she told of the bloody battles of her nation, particularly with the Americans; of the great prowess of her ancestors; their chivalrous exploits and "deeds of noble daring," or related some interesting events of her early life; her courtship and marriage; the great strength, bravery, and activity of her then young husband, Co-kun-di-aw-thah, and her own youthful charms. Her memory seemed a great storehouse out of which she brought "things new and old." In almost all her tales, however, whether tragic or mirthful, whether of great achievements in the battle and in the chase, or whether relating some diverting incident or humorous story, she mingled many superstitious ideas and spoke much of supernatural agency and of her own frequent intercourse and conversation with departed spirits. To the beaver she not only gave the faculty of reason, but the power of speech; and I shall ever recollect the song, said by her to have been sung by a beaver to an almost desponding hunter, stayed by a freshet and half starved; encouragingly telling him that the high waters would soon subside and that beyond the stream he would find plenty of game—

"Sawwattee sawwatty,
    Sawwattee sawwatty,
    Sawawkee meechee noo kakoohonny;
    Kooquay nippee ta tsa;
    Waugh waw waugh whaw,
    Waugh waw waugh whaw."

Cooh-coo-cheeh took much pains to teach me to dance; an accomplishment not so easily acquired as from the great simplicity of their steps might at first be supposed; grace with them consisting principally in the motions of the body; the action of their limbs being rather adapted to facilitate and perfect these (and not, as with us, at least in former days, the chief exhibitors of grace and skill) and it required much practice to combine both successfully. Having seen my elder instruct my younger sister in dancing, I had learned several steps, particularly the balancer and single and double chasser, and sometimes for the amusement of Cooh-coo-cheeh I gave her a specimen of the manner of our dancing. With the slower and more simple steps she seemed to be amused, occasionally laughing heartily at what to her appeared so ludicrous; but when I attempted a hornpipe, whirling around frequently, or capered along in a double chasser, so ridiculous did it appear to her, manifesting, as she thought, such a want of grace and dignity that usually with some marked expression of contempt she put a stop to my further exhibition.

Cooh-coo-cheeh was remarkably nice in her cookery, requiring her kettles to be scoured often and her bowls and spoons to be washed daily, and nothing offended her quicker than the appearance of sluttishness; and although I stood pretty high in her favor I sometimes incurred her displeasure by my neglect, particularly by my want of cleanliness, as she thought, in performing some of my household duties. On a very cold morning about the middle of January she had risen before day and, intending to make some hominy, had boiled the corn for some time with ashes to remove its hulls. It was my duty to cleanse it from the ashes, and as it had been long enough in them, I was ordered to get up and perform that duty. The old woman's temper was very quick and when roused she was like a fury; and by no means particular in selecting an instrument of punishment, when her poker was not at hand she seized a knife, axe, billet of wood, anything within her reach, hurling it at the unfortunate subject of her wrath. Not rising immediately, she uttered her customary "Oogh!" followed by a stroke of her poker, and not giving me time to put on my moccasins hurried me off with the kettle of boiling corn and a large coarse sieve to the river.

The Maumee had for some time been frozen over and through the ice, about six inches thick, we had cut and kept open a hole for the convenience of getting water. Placing the large sieve by the side of the opening and emptying the corn into it, I proceeded to dip up water, pouring it on the hominy, which I rubbed well to take off the hulls. I had not finished my work when my bare feet, all this time standing on the ice, were so pained with cold that I could endure it no longer, and stepping into the hominy was enjoying the luxury of its warmth when the old woman espied me. Calling me loudly by my Indian name, "Meecheway," and uttering several "ooghs," she ran down, furious with rage, to the river, and hurling her poker inflicted a severe blow on my back, felling me to the ice. Immediately, however, springing up I ran off, leaving her to finish the hominy, and did not return to the cabin until her anger had subsided.

CHAPTER IX

IT WAS NOW near the close of February, when sharp, frosty nights and days of warm sunshine succeeding the extreme cold of winter constituted what in early times in the West was called sugar weather; a season always improved by most families, who drew their year's supply from the sugar tree; and some made, besides, quantities of sugar for sale. Taking our large brass kettle with several small ones, some corn and beans for our sustenance, our bedding, and, indeed, all our household furniture and utensils excepting the hominy block, we closed our cabin door, placing the customary stick against it, crossed the Maumee below the mouth of the Auglaize, and packing our baggage on a horse proceeded four or five miles down the river to a beautiful open woods, principally of sugar trees intermixed with blue ash, elm, and poplar. Here Cooh-coo-cheeh had for many years made her sugar, and here we found a comfortable bark shelter with every convenience for sugar making save kettles, which we now supplied. I here found constant employment dusting out and setting the troughs, as the old woman tapped the trees; carrying the sap, cutting wood, making fires, and occasionally attending to boiling the water at night.

We had had a remarkably fine season and had been for several days employed, during which time we had collected sap sufficient to make, probably, a hundred weight of sugar, when one evening near sunset as we were quietly seated around the fire a messenger came and privately informed Cooh-coo-cheeh that the British agent from Detroit had arrived at Auglaize, and having purchased me of Mr. Ironside (who had been authorized by Wawpawmawquaw, now absent on a hunting expedition, to dispose of me) he had been sent to conduct me to the Point. Whether it was that she thought that the sudden joy which the news of my release from captivity would inspire might prove injurious to me, or whether she herself, having now become rather attached to me, was unwilling to part with me, the old woman received the intelligence (which she did not communicate to me until the next morning) with great seriousness, answering only with a simple "Hu! enee."

That evening she seemed more than usually disposed to converse with me, and repeating her inquiries about my parents, their rank in society, how long they had lived on the Ohio, and many such questions, asked me particularly of the place of their former residence; and when I told her that they once lived not far from the seashore, and near New York; and that their forefathers were English, who came from the Island on the eastern side of the great salt lake, south and east of us, her brow for a moment seemed deeply clouded and the mournful tones of her voice betrayed her mingled feeling of melancholy and regret. She spoke of the first landing of the "palefaces" from their monstrous canoes with their great white wings, as seen by her ancestors; of their early settlements, their rapid growth, their widely spreading population, their increasing strength and power, their insatiable avarice, and their continued encroachments on the red men; who, reduced by diseases, thinned by civil wars, and diminished by their long and various struggles, first with the British (Met-a-coo-se-a-qua) then with Se-mon-the (the Americans or Long-knives), were no longer powerful; and that they would not be satisfied until they had crowded the Indian to the extreme north to perish on the great ice lake; or to the far west until, pushing those who should escape from their rifles into the great waters, all would at length be exterminated. She spoke of the anger of the Great Spirit against the red men, especially those of her own nation, nearly all of whom had perished; and that herself and her children, the remnant of her race, would soon sleep in the ground, and that there would be none to gather them at the feast of the dead or to celebrate their obsequies.

But her countenance soon kindled with animation and her eyes sparkled with pleasure when, changing the mournful theme, she ended with a most glowing description of the beautiful hunting grounds, the ever-during abode of the brave and good red men. These she described as lying far, far beyond the vast western ocean, and as being ten-fold larger than the great continent of America. There, she said, the changing seasons brought no extremes of heat or cold, wet or drought; none were sick, none became old or infirm; and well do I recollect that, pointing to the large poplars near us, some of which were five or six feet in diameter and rose eighty feet without a limb, she spoke of the largest trees of that country as being twenty times larger and spreading their broad tops among the stars. Corn and beans and pumpkins and melons, she said, grew there spontaneously; the trees were loaded with the richest fruits; the ground was clothed were perpetual verdure, and the flowers on the prairies were everblooming and fragrant; the springs were abundant, clear, and cool; the rivers large, deep, and transparent, abounding with fish of endless varieties; the fine open woods were stocked with innumerable herds of buffaloes, deer, elk, and moose, and every species of game: in short there was a paradise containing all that could delight the mind or gratify the senses, and to crown all the exclusive home of the Indian. The little Canadian Frenchman, for such was the messenger, listened with that attention which among the Indians is inseparable from good manners; frequently expressing his admiration and even his wonder, though once or twice turning to me and smiling incredulously, he said, "Ma foi! dat is grand contry."

We arose early the next morning, when the Frenchman expressing his intention to set out immediately for the Point, Cooh-coo-cheeh, now for the first time communicating to me the information he had given her on the preceding night, told me that I should go down to Detroit, cross the great lake in a big canoe, and performing a large circuit arrive at my home on the Ohio. She spoke of the happiness of my family, especially the joy of my mother at my safe return; then of her own regret in parting with me, having, as she said, begun to regard me as her child; and concluded by saying that if I should grow up to be a man I must come and see her. She was affected even to tears as, taking my hands in both of hers and cordially pressing them, she bade me adieu. Poor Sotonegoo sobbed loudly as I took her hand and for the moment deeply affected, bade her farewell.

Leaving the cabin, I now followed the Frenchman at a brisk pace; frequently, however, looking back at its inmates, who were still standing near it, until the intervening trees hid them forever from my sight. It was a very pleasant morning on the last day of February, 1793, that I bade adieu to my Indian friends. The sun, just rising, seemed to shine with unusual splendor; never before, as I thought, had he appeared so bright and beautiful. I had been at first "as one that dreamed," scarcely crediting the fact that I was no longer a prisoner; gradually, however, as I left my late dwelling farther and farther behind me, becoming assured and conscious of the truth that I was indeed free, I was like a bird loosed from his cage or a young colt from his stall; to suppress my feelings or restrain my joy would have been almost impossible. I laughed, I wept, I whistled, I shouted and sung by turns; never had I moved with step so elastic; now skipping over logs, jumping, dancing, and running alternately, while the Frenchman (whose name I found on inquiry to be Joseph Blanche) sometimes stopped and looked at me as if suspecting that I was more than half insane. By degrees, however, this extreme of joy subsiding, I became more temperate, confining the expression of my happiness to singing and whistling, which I kept up almost without intermission until we reached the Auglaize, when, stepping into a canoe and crossing the river, in a few minutes we entered the hospitable dwelling of Mr. Ironside.

This gentleman received me with more than his usual kindness and congratulating me heartily on my release from Indian captivity introduced me to Colonel Elliott, the British Indian agent, and to a Mr. Sharp, a merchant of Detroit[25] who had accompanied him to Auglaize. Elliott received me with considerable hauteur, and with a look that spoke that his noticing me was condescension; and although, as I afterward learned, he had been sent by the express order of Governor Simcoe to effect my ransom and convey me to Detroit, yet, as if such a service was degrading, he pretended that being at Auglaize on public business he had accidentally heard of me and actuated wholly by motives of humanity procured my release, for which he had agreed to pay one hundred and twenty dollars. Having understood from Cooh-coo-cheeh that I was to be sent home to my parents, I was not a little disappointed in finding, as I supposed, that I was the property of an individual and subject to be disposed of at his pleasure; however, I soon comforted myself with the thought that the same humanity which had moved him to effect my ransom would influence him to perfect the generous act by restoring me to my friends, and that at the worst my condition would be greatly meliorated. Elliott, I have no doubt, had conveyed to Mr. Ironside the same false impression, that my ransom was altogether his own private affair; as that gentleman, equally scorning such pitiful deceit to magnify his generosity, as incapable of trifling with the feelings of one in my hapless situation, would had he known the truth have immediately undeceived me.

The wife of Ironside now kindly invited me to breakfast; but Elliott, objecting to the trouble it would give her, ordered Joseph to take me over to James Girty's, where he said our breakfast would be provided. Girty's wife soon furnished us with some coffee, wheat bread, and stewed pork and venison, of which (it being so much better than the food to which I had been lately accustomed) I ate with great *gout*; but I had not more than half breakfasted when Girty came in and seating himself opposite to me, said, "So, my young Yankee, you're about to start for home." I answered, "Yes, sir, I hope so." That, he said, would

---

[25]George Sharp was a prominent Detroit trader at this period. Notwithstanding the unattractive guise in which Spencer presents him he is described by William Robertson, a contemporary Detroit merchant, as being "of liberal education and highly respected." He died at Montreal in January, 1800.

depend on my master, in whose kitchen he had no doubt I should first serve a few years' apprenticeship as a scullion. Then taking his knife, said (while sharpening it on a whetstone), "I see your ears are whole yet, but I'm d--n--y mistaken if you leave this without the Indian mark, that we may know you when we catch you again." I did not wait to prove whether he was in jest or in downright earnest, but leaving my breakfast half finished, I instantly sprang from the table, leaped out of the door, and in a few seconds took refuge in Mr. Ironside's house. On learning the cause of my flight Elliott uttered a sardonic laugh, deriding my unfounded childish fears, as he was pleased to term them; but Ironside looked serious, shaking his head as if he had no doubt that if I had remained Girty would have executed his threat.

Everything being now ready for our departure, we took our leave of Mr. Ironside and his wife (I with feelings of gratitude for their kindness which I have never forgotten) and of several of the inhabitants on the Point, who wished us a good voyage and me a safe return home; and seating ourselves in a small open bateau, steered by Joseph and rowed by a stout Canadian whom he called Baptiste, we soon cleared the point and began to descend the Maumee. Passing the cabin of Cooh-coo-cheeh on its northern bank I took a last look at the spot where I had spent more than seven months of hopeless captivity and very many hours of painful solicitude and fearful apprehension. Nearly eight months before, I had arrived there, weary, exhausted, half famished, sick, desponding, and a prisoner, truly an object of pity; now, although ragged, dirty, bareheaded, and very much tanned, my looks were by no means inviting, still I enjoyed good health; and what with me seemed then to comprise almost every blessing, I was free from savage captivity. Turning my back forever upon my late residence, with tears of gratitude I devoutly thanked God for my deliverance; and as I thought that the ever-rolling current aided by every stroke of the oar was wafting me nearer and nearer home, I felt a pleasure which it would be impossible for me to describe.

Of Elliott and Sharp I have but an indistinct recollection: they were both men of only ordinary size, having nothing remarkable in their appearance. Elliott's hair was black, his complexion dark, his features small; his nose, I recollect, was short, turning up at the end, his look was haughty and his countenance repulsive; Sharp, on the contrary, had light hair and fair complexion, with a smirking look and a counte-nance indicative of shallowness. After an hour spent in light and unim-portant conversation Sharp, I suppose merely to pass away the time, requested me to relate the particulars of my captivity, with which, however, he appeared but little interested; often interrupting me to make some observation on persons or things as we passed down the river. He then made several inquiries about my family, the Miami settlements, and Fort Washington; which leading to a more general conversation, drew from Elliott many ungentlemanly remarks and disparaging observations about the Americans. Sharp then observed that being so full of notions of liberty and equality they would make rather stubborn servants, and he thought I would be no great bargain. "However," he continued, looking at me, "I suppose you will not have much employment for him?" "Not much," replied Elliott, "besides cleaning knives and forks, blacking shoes, running of errands, and waiting upon table." With an expression of disgust and indignation I turned my back upon him. The truth was, I more than half doubted his having more to do with me than to convey me to Detroit. I asked no more questions of either of them and when questioned answered as briefly as possible; amusing myself with looking at the numerous fish swimming in the clear stream or at the lofty trees, with here and there an Indian hut or village on its banks; and now listening to the cheerful song of the boatmen as the one plied his oar and the other his paddle, timing their strokes as exactly with their music as a soldier would the tread of his left foot with the flam of the drum.

On the first night after leaving the Auglaize we slept at a Wyandot village, and on the following morning, passing the rapids, we landed about the middle of the afternoon on the northern bank of the Maumee, a few miles above its entrance into Lake Erie, at a small encampment of Wyandots. Here the two boatmen with their bateau, leaving us, proceeded to their home at Frenchtown; and here Elliott, placing me in charge of the Wyandots, with whom he had contracted, probably for a gallon of rum, to convey me to Detroit, mounting his horse in company with Sharp, rode off, leaving me again to the mercy of the savages.

The Indians, eight or ten in number, commenced drinking pretty freely directly after Elliott left us, and soon becoming half drunk, began to sing and dance and shout and wrestle as usual. Among them was a youth of about fourteen, who, while I was sitting as a spectator on one side of the tent, came and pulling me up insisted that I should wrestle with him. This I refused, objecting to the great inequality of our years and size and strength; but being urged I at length consented, and as I was very strong for one of my years and withal quite active, in a very few seconds I laid him sprawling on the ground. In a second effort he was more successful, throwing me down; but the moment I struck the ground, giving a sudden spring I threw myself over him, and as he struggled by force to get up held him down until he asked me to let him rise.

Mortified and angry he now got up, and seizing me by the hair and passing his finger around my head, at the same time blackguarding me in broken Shawnee, said he would scalp me. That moment I gave him a severe blow in the pit of the stomach, which, while it made him loose his hold upon my hair, nearly knocked him down. I now stood in an attitude of defense, determined to resent or resist any further insult or violence; he did not now approach me, but waiting an opportunity when, supposing his anger had cooled, I had turned round and walked a few steps with the intention of sitting down, drew his knife and stealing behind me stabbed me in the back. He no doubt intended to inflict a mortal wound, but the knife, fortunately striking the lower part of my shoulder blade, glanced down across the ribs without entering the body, making an incision about an inch wide, and found, when afterwards probed by a British surgeon at Detroit, to be three inches deep.

An old Indian now interfered, and discovering from the blood that flowed that I was badly wounded, stripped off my capote and pressing the wound firmly, applied a large quid of tobacco to its orifice; then covering it with a compress secured by a bandage over my shoulder and round my chest, effectually staunched the blood. Early next morning (so great had been Elliott's care for me) I was confided to the charge of two old squaws, who, placing me in the middle of their canoe, set out for Detroit (about forty-five miles distant) and paddling along the edge of the lake and up the strait, arriving at that place on the evening of the third of March, delivered me to Colonel Richard England, the officer commanding that garrison.

CHAPTER X

COLONEL ENGLAND[26] HAD been instructed by Governor Simcoe to receive me, to provide clothing and everything necessary for my comfort, and to send me on to Fort Niagara as soon as the navigation of Lake Erie should open. He had, besides, been informed about my family, and particularly about my relatives; and was personally acquainted with some connections of my mother; so that from his sense of duty as well as from a disposition to oblige his friends I would have been assured of a favorable reception. But independently of these considerations, being both a gentleman and a man of great humanity he received me with much kindness and, regarding my wretched appearance with sympathy for my condition, followed only the generous impulse of his nature in ministering to my relief and comfort. After asking me some brief questions and kindly assuring me of my future welfare, addressing himself to Lieutenant Andre, an officer of the same regiment (who, also expecting me, had on hearing of my arrival repaired to the colonel's quarters), said he committed me to his charge, observing that Mr. Andre would of course take pleasure in making the necessary provision for me.

Mr. Andre immediately took me by the hand and led me to his quarters in the same barracks, only a few doors distant, and requesting me to sit down, retired from the apartment. In a few minutes a servant entered and set before me some tea and bread and butter, on which having supped, I arose and was retiring from the table when two women,

---

[26]Richard England, a native of Ireland, entered the British army in 1766 and died in 1812 with the rank of lieutenant-general. He was commandant at Detroit from 1792 until its transfer to the United States in 1796. His administration here seems to have given general satisfaction, even as his conduct won the praises of the lonely captive boy whose narrative we are following. Colonel England was a man of great size, being six and a half feet in height. The story is told that the Prince of Wales once inquired his name, and on being told, exclaimed: "England! He should be named Great Britain at least."

whom mere curiosity, as I supposed, had kept standing at one end of the room looking at me intently while I was eating, now advanced, and each unceremoniously taking me by the hand and leading me out of the apartment, conducted me to a chamber. Here, stripping off all but my shirt, carefully throwing my clothes out at a back window, beyond the palisades of the town, and seating me in a large washtub, half filled with water, they tore off my shirt, which had fast adhered to the bandage round my shoulder, before I had time to tell them I was wounded, and so suddenly, inflicting for a moment acute pain, as to extort from me a loud scream. Their surprise at this soon ceased when I told them that an Indian had stabbed me in the shoulder; and when they saw the blood from the open wound running down my back, one of them, alarmed, ran to inform Mr. Andre; the other, with a rag immediately staunching the blood, [proceeded] deliberately to scour my person with soap and water, and by the time the surgeon had arrived had effected a complete ablution. On probing the wound, which he found to be about three inches deep, the surgeon pronounced it to be not dangerous; fortunately, he said, the knife in entering had struck the lower posterior point of the right shoulder-blade, and taken a direction downward; but had it entered an inch lower or nearer the spine it would probably have caused death.

From the want of clothes it was late next morning before I could get up; but receiving at length a temporary supply of a roundabout and pantaloons from the wardrobe of Ensign O'Brian, brother of Mrs. England, and a pair of stockings and slippers from one of the women, I made my appearance in the breakfast room and was introduced to Mrs. Andre, wife of the lieutenant. She very kindly took my hand and congratulated me on my deliverance from the Indians; though she could not help smiling at my singular appearance, dressed, as I was, in clothes which although they fitted the smallest officer in the garrison hung like bags on me. Mrs. Andre made very particular inquiries about my mother (whose maiden name was Ogden) and my relatives on her side; and telling me that she had been a Miss Ogden, made our relationship to be that of third cousins.

This unexpected information gave me great pleasure; for to find among strangers and in highly polished society one who was not ashamed to acknowledge as a relative a destitute boy, far from friends and home, could not but be truly gratifying. But Mrs. Andre possessed none of the false pride of those who, governed wholly by factitious circumstances, while they "have respect to the man in gay clothing," feeling as if degraded by condescension to the unfortunate, say to the poor, "Stand thou there." She was kind and amiable, as she was handsome and accomplished; and although quite young, apparently not more than twenty, supplied to me the place of a mother. Her husband, a brother of the unfortunate Major Andre,[27] and one of the handsomest men I ever saw, very affable in his manners and frank in his disposition, treated me with great kindness; and after seeing that I was comfortably and, indeed, genteelly dressed, introduced me to the families of Mr. Erskine[28] and Commodore Grant[29] (where I found boys and girls of nearly my own age, who cheerfully associated with me) and took pleasure in showing me the town, the shipping, the fort, and whatever else he thought would afford me gratification.

The situation of Detroit on the western bank of the strait connecting Lake Huron with Lake Erie and about ten miles south of Lake St. Clair, is familiar to all; though but few here have any knowledge of what it was more than forty years since. It was then a small town containing only wooden buildings, but few of which were well finished; surrounded by high pickets inclosing an area of probably half a mile square, only one-third part of which, along the bank of the river (as the strait is called), was covered with houses. There were, I think, three narrow streets running parallel with the river, and intersected by four or five more at right angles. At the south end of the town, adjoining on the west the second street, at the ends of which were the entrances (secured by heavy wooden gates) into the city, was a space about two hundred feet square, inclosed on a part of two sides with low palisades, within which a row of handsome three-story barracks for the accommodation of the officers occupied the south side, and buildings of the same height for the soldiers' quarters stood on the west and a part of the north side. The

---

[27]Major Andre of Revolutionary fame had a younger brother, William Lewis, whom the *British Army List* for 1790 shows as a captain in the Twenty-sixth Infantry. In the Twenty-fourth Infantry (Colonel England's regiment) was a lieutenant, Charles S. Andrews. Probably the latter, rather than Major Andre's brother, was the officer who befriended Spencer.

[28]This was doubtless John Askin, a Scotch-Irishman who came to Detroit soon after the French and Indian War. He served the British government as commissary at Mackinac for a time, but was dismissed from this service in 1780 and spent the remainder of his career as a merchant and fur trader. When Detroit was given over to the United States in 1796 Askin, electing to remain a subject of Great Britain, removed to the Canadian side of the river, where he died in 1817. Several of his sons, the children with whom Spencer played, served in the War of 1812, and one of them, John Askin Jr., played a leading part in the capture of Mackinac from the Americans. The Askin family papers are preserved in the Burton Library at Detroit.

[29]Commodore Alexander Grant was a brother-in-law of John Askin. He had command of all the military shipping on the Great Lakes from 1763 until 1812. He was also for many years a member of the executive council of Upper Canada, and in 1805 was *de facto* governor of the province during the interregnum between Governors Hunter and Gore. He died at Grosse Pointe near Detroit in 1815.

open space was occupied as a parade ground, where the troops were every day exercised by the adjutant.

In the northwest corner of the large area, inclosed with pickets, on ground a little elevated, stood the fort, separated from the houses by an esplanade, and surrounding, first by an abatis of treetops having the butts of the limbs sharpened and projecting outward about four feet high; then by a deep ditch, in the center of which were high pickets; and then by a row of light palisades seven or eight feet long, projecting horizontally from the glacis. The fort, covering not more than half an acre of ground, was square, having a bastion at each angle, with parapets and ramparts so high as to shelter the quarters within, which were bombproof entirely from the shot of an enemy. Its entrance was on the east side facing the river, over a drawbridge, and through a covered way; over which on each side were long iron cannon carrying twenty-four pound shot, and which the officers called the "British lions"; while on each of the other sides were planted two, and on each bastion four, cannon of various caliber: six, nine, and twelve pounders.

The fort was garrisoned by a company of artillery under the command of Captain Spears, [30] while two companies of infantry and one of grenadiers of the Twenty-fourth (Colonel England's regiment) were quartered in the barracks; the balance of the regiment was at Michilimakinak and other northern posts. By the side of the gate near the end of the officers' barracks was a twenty-four pounder; and for the protection of the east side of the town there were two small batteries of cannon on the bank of the river. In the spring of 1793 there were anchored in the river in front of the town three brigs of about two hundred tons each; the *Chippewa* and the *Ottawa*, new vessels, carrying each, I think, eight guns; the *Dunmore*, an old vessel of six guns; and a sloop, the *Felicity*, of about one hundred tons, armed only with two swivels; all belonging to His Majesty, George III, and commanded by Commodore Grant. There were, besides, several merchantmen, sloops, and schooners, the property of individuals. [31]

---

[30]In 1794, Captain Spears was at Fort Miamis on the Maumee, the fortification newly established by the British as an offset to the American advance. When after the battle of Fallen Timbers Wayne's soldiers pursued the fleeing red men to the walls of the fort and destroyed the adjoining houses and property of the British traders under its guns, the British commander sent Captain Spears with a message of inquiry and remonstrance concerning Wayne's acts and intentions.

[31]The early history of shipping on the Great Lakes is still shrouded in obscurity. Spencer's information about the vessels at Detroit in 1792 is perhaps as authoritative as any we have. The sloop *Felicity* had been on the lakes for at least a dozen years. An account of a cruise taken in

I had spent almost four weeks very agreeably at Detroit, becoming much attached to Colonel England and particularly so to Mr. and Mrs. Andre, who treated me with great kindness, and to the family of Mr. Erskine, who were very friendly and polite to me; and when, near the close of March the lake being entirely clear of ice; and when, though there was some danger to be apprehended from easterly storms it was thought that the navigation to Fort Erie would be tolerably safe, orders were issued for the sailing of the *Felicity*, I felt a momentary regret that I was so soon to be separated from these kind friends and acquaintances. Everything being in readiness and the sloop beginning to weigh anchor, I took leave of Mr. and Mrs. Andre, thanking them with tears for their parental kindness; and so affected was I that I could scarcely pronounce the word farewell. Of Colonel England, also, who wished me a prosperous voyage and safe return to my friends, I took a very affecting leave, acknowledging with gratitude my obligations to him; then with a small bundle containing a few shirts and stockings, accompanying the sailor who was waiting to conduct me, proceeded to the sloop's boat and in a few minutes more was safe on board the *Felicity*.

With a light breeze we proceeded down the strait; but the wind being from the southwest we went but little faster than the current, as we were obliged to tack very frequently from side to side of the river. Anchoring at its mouth, we lay there during the night; and the next morning, the wind freshening a little from the same direction, we were enabled in addition to our lower sails to spread our top sail and top gallant sail, and about the middle of the afternoon anchored in Put-in-bay, a fine harbor in the western part of Lake Erie, formed by the North, Middle, and South Bass, the Strentian and some smaller islands.

The wind being light and variable and there being some appearance of a change of weather, Captain Fleming[32] thought it most prudent to remain here until morning; and taking me into the boat with two oarsmen and a couple of hooks and lines, rowed round the bay trailing the lines from the stern. Passing along the northern side of Strentian

---

her around Lake Michigan in 1779 is published in *Wisconsin Historical Collections*, XI, 203–12. The *Dunmore* was built at Detroit in 1774. According to an official return of 1783 she was a seventy-ton vessel, carrying ten guns and twenty-five seamen. The same document gives the *Felicity* as a forty-five ton vessel. Interesting accounts of early shipping on the Great Lakes may be found in the Buffalo Historical Society, *Publications*, VI, 17–33 and VIII, 283 ff.

[32]Probably Lieutenant Fleming of the Marine service. From the *Michigan Pioneer and Historical Collections* we learn that in 1798 he had a large family at Amherstburg (opposite Detroit) and that in 1803 he was relieved of the command of his vessel because of insanity.

Island, which is convex, steep, and rocky, we caught several fine bass (one of which I had the pleasure of drawing into the boat) on which we made a delicious meal.

On a high rocky point of this island stood a very large, tall tree towering above the adjacent woods, on the top of which was an aerie. Here first I saw the noble American eagle and amused myself for some time watching several of them, as without the least apparent exertion they gracefully, yet with amazing velocity, compassed the bay; gradually rising and contracting their sphere with each circuit until, suddenly mounting, they seemed a mere speck in the blue sky; then as suddenly descending almost with the rapidity of thought to mid-air, they began to wheel around, doubling their sphere with each circuit as they descended, some lighting on the trees, others darting on their prey. One of them lighted on the high tree near the nest, where his mate could be seen, probably hatching her eggs, and whose place he took soon after as she left her nest for food or recreation.

Early next morning, it being the first day of April, having a light breeze from the south we weighed anchor and sailing eastwardly in a few hours passed between Point Pelee and Middle Islands; and at four o'clock in the afternoon (our sloop being a pretty good sailer) had made about fifty miles, when the wind, suddenly coming round, began to blow fresh from the east. We continued onward, however, regularly tacking from southeast to northeast as near to the wind as the vessel would progress until after sunset, the wind still increasing. We were now out of sight of land; the water all around us seeming to touch the horizon and the curling waves crested with foam appearing to mingle with the clouds, presented to me a novel, sublime, and yet fearful spectacle.

I had retired to my berth on the larboard side of the cabin about ten o'clock and notwithstanding the noise of the waves and the pitching of the vessel had fallen into a sound sleep, when the wind having increased to a tempest, to proceed was impossible. For some time we lay to under a close-reefed jib and mainsail, when the captain, seeing no prospect of the storm's abating and fearing that the rolling of the sloop would unship her mast, gave orders to put her about. In coming round on the starboard we were nearly upset; I was awakened by being thrown from my berth against the opposite side of the cabin; and the next moment a heavy sea, striking the stern and forcing in the cabin windows, poured in several hogsheads of water, in which, tossed about from side to side, it was nearly a minute before I could gain my feet and ascend to the deck. The dead lights were, however, soon closed and the vessel cleared of water, and I was advised by the captain to return to my berth in the cabin; but I preferred remaining on deck, thinking that if the sloop should be wrecked I should have a much better chance of escape. Although scudding almost under bare poles (merely carrying sail enough to steer the vessel by) we were going at the rate of twelve knots an hour and pitching and rolling with the heavy swells, sometimes fearing that we should lose our mast or that the seams of the vessel (rather old and unseaworthy) opening, she would flounder; or, the lake being shallow, that she would be dashed to pieces against the bottom. Providence, however, kindly preserved us, and just after daylight, passing the fearful breakers on the north side of Point Pelee, we soon anchored safely in Put-in-bay. Tom, the cook, who was held as an oracle on board the sloop, openly declared that our being driven back by the storm was in consequence of our sailing from the bay on Friday, being, besides, the first day of April, to which all the crew assented, adding that we were lucky in getting safely back.

We spent a part of Saturday afternoon in an excursion through the Middle Bass Island on which we killed several large rattlesnakes. I narrowly escaped being bitten by one at least three feet long over which I stepped as he crossed the path; and the captain, who had gone to a small pond a few hundred yards ahead of us to shoot ducks, returned in a short time running and out of breath, declaring that a monster, a snake more than a rod in length, the moment he fired at some ducks issued from the long grass by the edge of the water, made directly toward him, and pursued him for more than twenty rods. On our return to the sloop we caught some fine bass, which more than compensated us for the loss of the captain's ducks.

The next morning being Sunday, having the wind fresh from the south and the weather being favorable, we again weighed anchor and stood out of the bay, Tom prognosticating that we should have a prosperous voyage. His predictions seemed likely to be verified, as we sailed finely this day; Tom entertained us with several marvelous stories and extraordinary adventures of which he had a store, and of which many would compare with those of "Sinbad the Sailor"; besides, he had a great variety of nautical songs, some of which, as "Sweet Poll of Plymouth" and "All in the Downs," he sang with considerable pathos; and others, of bloody battles and brilliant victories, he sang with great spirit; but none of my entreaties could prevail with him to sing "Cease, Rude Boreas," which he said was to be sung only on shore over a good can of grog, in company with wives and sweethearts.

The wind, which had been favorable all day Sunday, veered round before Monday morning, blowing very fresh directly ahead; and soon after daylight, when in sight of Long or Puttshawk's Point and not much more than a hundred miles from Lake Erie, to our great disappointment a storm even more furious than the first compelled us to put about and drove us quite back to Put-in-bay, which we reached on Monday evening. On Wednesday morning we again sailed, and on the day following were again driven back by a furious storm, which carried away our top gallant mast. On returning this time I was extremely sick from the pitching and rolling of the sloop, and began to be discouraged, fearing we should never get across the lake.

We had in the hold of the sloop an ill-looking man, said to be an American, whom the British had taken up at Detroit on suspicion of his being a spy; and on whose person some papers said to be plans of the fort and town were found. Pronouncing him guilty, Colonel England had ordered him to be heavily ironed and put on board the sloop to be conveyed to Niagara. Tom now declared this man was a Jonah, on whose account the vessel had not been permitted to cross the lake. One who, though he had escaped justice on shore, the Almighty would not suffer to reach the land alive; and so deeply were the crew imbued with this sentiment that but for a discovery made on the following day they might have been tempted to execute their threats, which they had privately made, to throw him overboard.

On Friday morning, the wind being still from the east, the captain proposed that we should go a-fishing and then make a little excursion through the North Bass Island. Making a compass round westerly and northerly in our boat, catching a few fine bass, a moderate sized sturgeon, and some white fish, we proceeded to the middle of the south side of the North Bass Island, and crossing it in a northeasterly direction to its north shore were attracted to a spot a few hundred yards west of us by a great number of buzzards, some on the ground and others sitting on the trees or flying around in the air. Approaching the place, we saw a light bateau-fashioned canoe, split and shattered, lying on the top of the bank just in the edge of the woods; and looking about a few minutes, found not far from the canoe a man in a high state of putrefaction, who had been drowned probably a week before in attempting to cross from Point Au Plait to the bay. His face and neck were entirely destroyed by the buzzards; but from his dress, a drab-colored capote, overalls, and moccasins, and his skin, seen by opening his calico shirt, it was evident that he was a Canadian Frenchman.

The cause of our detention and our having been repeatedly driven back by storms was immediately explained by Tom, who, declaring that the Almighty would not suffer us to cross the lake while this man lay unburied instantly began preparations for his interment. Taking the poor Frenchman's paddle which lay near him, aided by another sailor, sometimes with a stick and sometimes with his hands, in about an hour a grave two feet deep was dug in the soft sandy ground on the top of the bank, into which the corpse, dragged up by the shoulders, being placed, Tom drew from his pocket a prayer book and opening it at the burial service, handed it to the captain, who read it with great solemnity. The grave was now filled up, the paddle with its blade upward was planted at its head, and over it were thrown brush and logs for its protection; when, satisfied that we had done a good work, we returned to our boat and on board the sloop, where Tom, having in about an hour prepared us an excellent dinner of fish and potatoes, we ate with great *gout*, our appetites, from the exercise of the morning, being very keen.

The wind still continued to blow strongly from the east and the lake outside of the bay was very rough; but on Wednesday, the thirteenth of April, the one changing to the southeast and the other becoming calm, we again set sail, and on Friday evening anchored safely opposite to Fort Erie. On the following morning taking leave of the sloop's crew I went on shore with the captain, who introduced me to the officer commanding the fort, at the same time delivering him a letter written by Colonel England. I was detained here only a few hours, when, being placed on board a small barge in charge of a corporal and four soldiers, I was in a few hours conveyed to Fort Chippewa, a blockhouse garrisoned by a lieutenant and thirty men on the north side of Chippewa Creek, a few rods from its mouth and about two miles above the falls of Niagara.

Here passing the night, on the following morning, accompanied by a man whom the lieutenant had provided to conduct me I walked down to the falls, and after spending about two hours in viewing that stupendous cataract proceeded to Queenstown, where finding a wood boat going down to Fort Niagara, I immediately got on board, and arriving there an hour after and delivering a letter to the commanding officer, was by him conducted to the quarters of Lieutenant Hill, where I was received with great kindness.

CHAPTER XI

FORTY YEARS SINCE, the southwestern part of the state of New York was almost an unbroken wilderness; and excepting a log ferry-house on the top of a high bank opposite Queenstown (near the present site of Lewiston) there was but one house on the road or rather footpath between Niagara and Canandaigua, a distance of a hundred miles, and that was a tavern near the western bank of the Genesee, probably ten miles south of the spot where Rochester now stands. The best mode of traveling then was on horseback; but as there was but little communication between the western part of New York and Niagara, opportunities such as would be suitable for my return to my friends seldom occurred. I had, therefore, to wait patiently until such opportunity should offer, or until Governor Simcoe should provide some mode of conveyance. However, I was very comfortably situated in the family of Mr. Hill, and spent my time quite pleasantly for about a week that I remained at the fort. Lieutenant Hill was adjutant of the Fiftieth regiment of infantry, a part of which with a company of artillery garrisoned Fort Niagara, and a part was stationed at York, Upper Canada, on the west side of the lake, nearly opposite. Frequently by his invitation I accompanied him when he marched the troops not on duty out of the garrison, which he did on every fair day for the purpose of exercising them.

It is astonishing to see with what precision the British regulars go through the manual exercise, march and perform the different military evolutions and how quickly the slightest error or fault is noticed by the officer, who not infrequently punishes the delinquent by a stroke of his rattan over the knuckles or on the shins. The troops here, though almost perfectly disciplined were, I thought, inferior to the Twenty-fourth; who, beside, made a much more showy and as I conceived a more martial appearance. The uniform of the Twenty-fourth was a white vest and pantaloons with black half gaiters; a long scarlet coat faced with deep green and laced with silver at the button-holes, skirts, and wrists.

That of the Fiftieth was drab underclothes and long scarlet coats faced with light green without any ornament. The former wore their hair long, powdered, clubbed at the neck, and spreading like a fan between their shoulders; the latter had their hair cued.

With Mr. Hill I was much pleased. He appeared to be what is generally termed a clever man; plain yet urbane in his manners—not brilliant. His principal recommendation was his natural kindness and frankness, his sociability as a companion, and his punctual observance of his duty as an officer. Being at least fifteen years younger than his wife, whom he treated rather with deference than with affection, I think it probable that fortune, rank, or some consideration other than love influenced his union with her. His wife was at least forty; tall and lean, with large and homely features; in her dress very neat and simple; polished, though rather precise in her manners; quite intelligent and fluent, and possessing a very amiable disposition. During my stay with her she treated me with the kindness of a mother, carefully repairing my shirts and clothes: and when I left her, presenting me with a calico needle and thread case, that I might learn to mend my own clothes when occasion should require. This I carefully preserved for many years, often finding it useful: and from the habit formed when young have ever since carried a needle and thread in my pocket book: and often thus have been led gratefully to remember that benevolent lady.

The situation of Fort Niagara was a very commanding one, standing on the high bank at the mouth of the strait connecting Lakes Erie and Ontario: and the scenery around it was at once romantic, grand, and sublime. Above were the high precipitous banks or rather mountains, covered to the water's edge with trees and huge masses of rock, between which the broad and mighty water contracted below the deafening cataract into a comparatively narrow stream, boiling and foaming and whirling along the mighty chasm, rushed for several miles with resistless impetuosity. A few miles below on the Canadian side seemingly hanging on the face of the mountainous bank, stood the large white mess house and quarters of the Queen's Rangers, constituting the principal buildings of Queenstown, and on a small plain between the termination of this hill and the lake shore was the small but neat village of Newark, then the residence of Governor Simcoe. On the west and north and east the dark deep waters of Ontario presented a vast expanse bounded only by the horizon, and inspired the beholder with mingled wonder, delight, and awe.

Here, especially in the "still night," you might hear the deep heavy roar of the mighty cataract, as the coming of the desolating tornado; and, indeed, it may be heard distinctly "as the sound of many waters" on

Lake Erie, more than twenty miles distant. I shall never forget the sensations with which I first heard it: sensations growing more and more intense as I approached nearer and nearer to it: nor the feeling of apprehension with which while passing down the rapid current of the river I bent my body instinctively to the shore as if to make the boat cling to it. Glancing the eye from the first small break of the water (close to the British shore, just above the head of the long narrow island extending almost from the mouth of Chippewa to the falls, and at the foot of which formerly there was a small mill) in the direction of Goat Island to the middle of the river, you are struck with dread as you mark the second break, as it is called, where a part of the mighty river, sweeping down a steep ledge of rock, rises and rolls in fearful swells that threaten instant destruction. But no language can describe the feelings of the beholder when standing just in front of the awful precipice he first sees the vast volume of water rushing over, far beyond the angular summit rock (its upper bed) extending from its western bank to Goat Island, and plunging down, down into the deep abyss; then measures with his eye the giddy height of the foot of that island, rising perpendicularly from the depths below and presenting a face of solid rock; then views the beautiful unbroken sheet of water that falls between it and the eastern bank, facing the west and in front of which in clear, warm sunshine may be always seen a brilliant rainbow, with its ample arch spanning its width; then the troubled water, rising and bounding from its fearful plunge, back to the foot of the tremendous cataract, there forced again into the dread abyss, again emerging, rolls tumultuously down, a mighty torrent. But I had not intended to have attempted even this faint outline of this most grand, sublime, and wonderful of nature's works, to describe which would require the pen of a Milton; and in beholding which the mind is led involuntarily to exclaim, "Great and marvelous are Thy works, Lord God Almighty!"

I had been about a week at Fort Niagara when one afternoon Mr. Hill informed me that, an opportunity offering for me to return to my friends, Governor Simcoe had directed that I should immediately be sent over to Newark. Tying up my small wardrobe in my handkerchief in a few minutes I was ready to comply with this brief notice; then taking a hasty leave of Mr. and Mrs. Hill I was soon conveyed across the Niagara and conducted to the house of Governor Simcoe. The governor received me with great courtesy, and introducing me to Thomas Morris Esq. of Canandaigua,[33] who had arrived at Newark only the day

---

[33]This was Thomas Morris, son of Robert Morris of Philadelphia, the financier of the

before, remarked that he had acquainted that gentleman with the request that had been made to him by the British minister (at the instance of my friends) to ascertain where I was and to release me from captivity, and of the fortunate result of his efforts; and concluded by saying that Mr. Morris, on his request, had kindly consented to take me as far as Canandaigua. Mr. Morris then made some inquiries about my family and relatives: said he was well acquainted with my uncle, Colonel Ogden of Elizabethtown, New Jersey; that he would with pleasure convey me to Canandaigua, whence he had no doubt I would have an opportunity of returning to my friends.

In answering the inquiries made of me by Governor Simcoe I was led to speak of the conduct of Colonel Elliott; particularly of his leaving me in charge of the Indians at the mouth of the Maumee, and of the injury I had suffered and of the danger I had in consequence incurred. On hearing this he appeared to be quite indignant; he spoke of his instructions to Elliott to convey me to Detroit; and I well recollect his remark to Mr. Morris that such conduct in a British officer would have subjected him to trial before a court martial; but that he was obliged to overlook many improprieties in the agents, who had such influence with the Indians and were so necessary to His Majesty in his intercourse with them.

Mr. Morris now remarking that he proposed to set off from the ferry-house early next morning and that he would wait for me until next evening at Queenstown, arose and took his leave. Of Governor Simcoe's person, I have not a distinct recollection. I remember, however, that his figure was commanding, his features were manly, his countenance was open, his manners, though dignified, were affable; and in his conversation he had all the frankness of the soldier. I had the honor of taking tea that afternoon with his lady, a very handsome and intelligent woman, but unfortunately afflicted with so great an impediment in her speech that to me it was painful to converse with her.

After tea a servant appeared at the gate with two fine bay horses, on one of which after taking leave of Governor Simcoe and his lady I mounted, when the servant receiving his orders, "Spin him along," we set off at a rapid canter, and traveling at half speed up hill and down, in

---

American Revolution. In 1790 Robert Morris bought a tract of 1,267,000 acres of land in western New York from Phelps and Gorham, partners, who had obtained title from the state of Massachusetts. Morris shortly sold his land to a syndicate of English capitalists, but his son, Thomas, nevertheless came to Canandaigua to reside in 1792, making the place his permanent home. At the time of his hospitality to Spencer he was both a new resident of Canandaigua and a young man, being about twenty-three years of age.

less than an hour arrived at Queenstown. Crossing the Niagara about dusk and ascending the high bank, Mr. Morris and I entered the ferry-house where we found Mr. Nathaniel Gorham (if I mistake not, one of the proprietors of Canandaigua) and a colored servant who had traveled with him to the frontier. Here we spent the night, and on the next morning after a very early breakfast set out on horseback (a separate horse being provided for me) for Canandaigua. Traveling rapidly and stopping only an hour at noon to bait our horses and take a luncheon of biscuit and cheese, we rested at night at an Indian village; and on the next day, dining at about twelve o'clock at a tavern near the west bank of the Genesee, arrived at Canandaigua a little after dark; thus performing a journey of nearly a hundred miles through the wilderness, along a footpath, in two days.

Here I was placed in the family of Mr. Sanford, a tavernkeeper, with whom Mr. Morris (being then single, and not having quite finished his large and elegant house at the west end of the town) boarded. Canandaigua was, in 1793, a neat village, containing, I think, about forty houses scattered along the principal street leading westwardly from the long narrow lake after which it was named for more than a mile. At the head of this street facing the lake stood the house of Mr. Sanford, a large two-story wooden building, painted white and making a very respectable appearance. Near this house on the north was the village schoolhouse, where Mr. Upham taught about forty girls and boys; and below it was the residence of Mr. Chapin, agent for the Senecas, the eldest of whose sons traded with the Indians, exchanging his goods for furs and skins; while a younger one acted as an interpreter.

At Canandaigua I remained until about the middle of June, waiting for an opportunity to go to New York: at which time Mr. Chapin, having collected a large quantity of furs and bear and deer skins sufficient to load a pretty large bateau, being ready to set out for New York to replenish his stock of goods, at the request of Mr. Morris consented to take me with him. I had spent my time very pleasantly at Canandaigua, where I had employed a part of my time at school with Mr. Upham, and occasionally had amused myself in fishing at the outlet of the lake. I had been treated, too, by Mr. and Mrs. Sanford with parental kindness; but never from a stranger did I receive such benevolent and generous treatment as I received from Mr. Morris. He had incurred the expense of purchasing a horse to convey me from Niagara; he had defrayed the charge of my boarding and schooling at Canandaigua; he had furnished me with some summer clothing, and now that I was ready to set out for New York supplied me with money to bear my expenses; and for all this he would never afterwards receive the least remuneration.

I was deeply affected when I took my leave of him, and to this day when I think of him it is with feelings of the liveliest gratitude. Our bateau lay in the outlet about three miles north of the north end of Canandaigua Lake, to which point there was water sufficient for bateau navigation. From this point, having loaded the bateau with peltries conveyed in wagons from the village, we proceeded slowly down the narrow winding outlet; sometimes being obliged to stop and cut away trees that had fallen across it, and sometimes to get out and drag our flat-bottomed boat over the ripples. In this way we proceeded for nearly four days; passing, however, the several outlets of the Seneca and Cayuga, the Owasca, and other lakes, the stream gradually became larger and its obstructions fewer. On the fourth day we arrived at the mouth of the Oneida outlet, here called Three River Point, distant from Canandaigua by land about sixty miles, but at least one hundred by water. Ascending the outlet, we crossed the Oneida lake, about thirty miles in length, to the mouth of Wood Creek, up which small crooked stream we with much difficulty forced our bateau to within a mile of the Mohawk, whence transporting it across the ground where Rome now stands, but where then, on the Mohawk, stood but a solitary house, we proceeded down that river to Schenectady. From this place (Mr. Chapin conveying his peltries in wagons) we rode to Albany; whence, having stayed a day or two, we embarked on board a Dutch sloop for New York, where we arrived on the second day of July.

Here I took leave of Mr. Chapin, and on the next day, taking a passage in an open ferry boat (the only ferry boats in use at that time) across the bay, in which by a sudden gust of wind we were nearly upset, I arrived at Elizabethtown, New Jersey, where my sister and relations were delighted to see me. But the happiness I experienced in returning to the home of my childhood, after an absence of nearly three years in which I had endured so many privations and hardships and encountered so many dangers, must have been far superior to theirs; and when on the evening of that day I retired to rest, gratefully reflecting on the past goodness and mercy of God to me, devoutly, on my knees, I thanked Him for the exercise of His gracious providence toward me, preserving, sustaining, and protecting me and restoring me in safety to my friends.

The next day being the fourth of July, there was a very splendid celebration at Elizabethtown, which I enjoyed very much. At this time I had the pleasure of seeing my distant relative, the late Governor Bloomfield,[34] who was highly gratified with the narrative of my captivity and my account of Indian manners and customs, and took great pleasure in hearing my Indian songs, and in seeing me dance after the Indian mode. On the next

---

[34]Joseph Bloomfield, a native of New Jersey, served in the Revolution and in the War of 1812, attaining the rank of brigadier-general. He was at different times attorney-general of New Jersey, governor of the State, and representative in Congress.

day he caused to be published in *Kollock's New Jersey Journal* in substance the following notice: "Arrived at this place on the third instant, by the way of Detroit, Niagara, and New York, the only son of Colonel Oliver Spencer, late a captive among the Indians, with whom he remained about eight months, acquiring a considerable knowledge of their language, customs and manners." I think, too, that there was some allusion to my looks and manners, as slightly resembling the Indians.

This notice brought people from far and near to see me; some, no doubt, merely from the regard they bore to an old and esteemed friend or acquaintance, whose son I was; but the greater part from mere curiosity, as they would flock to an exhibition of wild beasts, expecting, no doubt, to see something at least half savage. At first I took pleasure in giving an account of my captivity; in answering the numerous inquiries that were made of me, and in singing and dancing Indian and uttering the various Indian yells; performing so naturally, as they supposed, and exhibiting as they fancied such a wildness in my looks and manners, that some frequently remarked in an undertone, "How much he looks like an Indian!" But being obliged to repeat the same story and answer the same questions frequently twenty times a day to different companies and individuals, I became so heartily tired of it that at last I gave only brief answers, often uttering a simple "Yes" or "No" to the inquiries that were made of me. Indeed, from the circumstance of then repeating so often the story of my captivity, and for weeks answering so many inquiries, I became averse to saying anything about it, and acquired a habit of replying so laconically to questions asked me that in after life I have felt mortified, when by my brief answers to questions on this subject I have seemed to check further inquiry and to give room to suspect me of want of politeness or even of civility.

My long narrative which must have exercised the patience of the reader, if indeed, he has taken time to read the whole of the preceding chapters of it, may soon be brought to a close. At Elizabethtown I remained with my sister and brother-in-law, Mr. Halstead, for a little more than a year, a regular portion of all of which time was occupied by me at school; and on the fourteenth of September, 1794, being then fourteen years old, I set out on horseback, in company with a Mr. Crane and the late General Schenck[35] (then on his first visit to the

---

[35]General William C. Schenck migrated to Ohio from New Jersey in 1793, settling first at Marietta. He soon removed to Cincinnati and shortly thereafter surveyed and founded the town of Franklin, Warren County. He served as an officer under General Harrison in the northwestern campaigns, and died in 1821. Two of his sons became prominent: Robert C. Schenck as Civil War general, member of Congress, and United States minister to Great Britain; and James F. Schenck as admiral in the United States navy.

West) on my return home. We performed the journey to Pittsburgh in ten days, and there putting our horses on board a flatboat descended the Ohio and arrived at Columbia about the middle of October. The joy of my parents on seeing me is more easily imagined than described; with tears and embraces they welcomed my return. The day was spent in affectionate inquiries about the past; and devoutly and gratefully that evening, around our family altar, did we join in thanksgiving and praise with my pious father to the Father of Mercies for all His past unmerited goodness; particularly for my preservation, and safe restoration to my home.

Nearly forty years have since passed away; our rivers teem with commerce; their banks are covered with farms, with houses, villages, towns, and cities; the wilderness has been converted into fruitful fields; temples to God are erected where once stood the Indian wigwam, and the praises of the Most High resound where formerly the screams of the panther or the yell of the savage only were heard. O, "what hath God wrought!" But where are the friends and companions of our youth? Our parents, where are they? Mine have long since "slept with their fathers." Wawpawmawquaw, who only a short time since had for several years previously paid me an annual visit, has gone to the land of his fathers, and almost all of those of whom in my narrative I have spoken are no longer "dwellers upon earth." We, also, will soon end our earthly pilgrimage and enter into "that bourne whence no traveler returns." May we through Divine grace "finish well our journey," that we may dwell at last where "ever-during spring abides, and never-withering flowers"; in that healthful clime where "sickness, sorrow, pain, and death are felt and feared no more"; where "there is fullness of joy," and where there are "pleasures forevermore."

INDEX

A CATALOG OF SELECTED
DOVER BOOKS
IN ALL FIELDS OF INTEREST

A CATALOG OF SELECTED DOVER
BOOKS IN ALL FIELDS OF INTEREST

CONCERNING THE SPIRITUAL IN ART, Wassily Kandinsky. Pioneering work by father of abstract art. Thoughts on color theory, nature of art. Analysis of earlier masters. 12 illustrations. 80pp. of text. 5⅜ × 8½. 23411-8 Pa. $3.95

ANIMALS: 1,419 Copyright-Free Illustrations of Mammals, Birds, Fish, Insects, etc., Jim Harter (ed.). Clear wood engravings present, in extremely lifelike poses, over 1,000 species of animals. One of the most extensive pictorial sourcebooks of its kind. Captions. Index. 284pp. 9 × 12. 23766-4 Pa. $11.95

CELTIC ART: The Methods of Construction, George Bain. Simple geometric techniques for making Celtic interlacements, spirals, Kells-type initials, animals, humans, etc. Over 500 illustrations. 160pp. 9 × 12. (USO) 22923-8 Pa. $8.95

AN ATLAS OF ANATOMY FOR ARTISTS, Fritz Schider. Most thorough reference work on art anatomy in the world. Hundreds of illustrations, including selections from works by Vesalius, Leonardo, Goya, Ingres, Michelangelo, others. 593 illustrations. 192pp. 7⅛ × 10¼. 20241-0 Pa. $8.95

CELTIC HAND STROKE-BY-STROKE (Irish Half-Uncial from "The Book of Kells"): An Arthur Baker Calligraphy Manual, Arthur Baker. Complete guide to creating each letter of the alphabet in distinctive Celtic manner. Covers hand position, strokes, pens, inks, paper, more. Illustrated. 48pp. 8¼ × 11. 24336-2 Pa. $3.95

EASY ORIGAMI, John Montroll. Charming collection of 32 projects (hat, cup, pelican, piano, swan, many more) specially designed for the novice origami hobbyist. Clearly illustrated easy-to-follow instructions insure that even beginning papercrafters will achieve successful results. 48pp. 8¼ × 11. 27298-2 Pa. $2.95

THE COMPLETE BOOK OF BIRDHOUSE CONSTRUCTION FOR WOOD-WORKERS, Scott D. Campbell. Detailed instructions, illustrations, tables. Also data on bird habitat and instinct patterns. Bibliography. 3 tables. 63 illustrations in 15 figures. 48pp. 5¼ × 8½. 24407-5 Pa. $1.95

BLOOMINGDALE'S ILLUSTRATED 1886 CATALOG: Fashions, Dry Goods and Housewares, Bloomingdale Brothers. Famed merchants' extremely rare catalog depicting about 1,700 products: clothing, housewares, firearms, dry goods, jewelry, more. Invaluable for dating, identifying vintage items. Also, copyright-free graphics for artists, designers. Co-published with Henry Ford Museum & Greenfield Village. 160pp. 8¼ × 11. 25780-0 Pa. $9.95

HISTORIC COSTUME IN PICTURES, Braun & Schneider. Over 1,450 costumed figures in clearly detailed engravings—from dawn of civilization to end of 19th century. Captions. Many folk costumes. 256pp. 8⅜ × 11¾. 23150-X Pa. $10.95

FRANK LLOYD WRIGHT'S HOLLYHOCK HOUSE, Donald Hoffmann. Lavishly illustrated, carefully documented study of one of Wright's most controversial residential designs. Over 120 photographs, floor plans, elevations, etc. Detailed perceptive text by noted Wright scholar. Index. 128pp. 9¼ × 10¾.
27133-1 Pa. $11.95

THE MALE AND FEMALE FIGURE IN MOTION: 60 Classic Photographic Sequences, Eadweard Muybridge. 60 true-action photographs of men and women walking, running, climbing, bending, turning, etc., reproduced from rare 19th-century masterpiece. vi + 121pp. 9 × 12. 24745-7 Pa. $10.95

1001 QUESTIONS ANSWERED ABOUT THE SEASHORE, N. J. Berrill and Jacquelyn Berrill. Queries answered about dolphins, sea snails, sponges, starfish, fishes, shore birds, many others. Covers appearance, breeding, growth, feeding, much more. 305pp. 5¼ × 8¼. 23366-9 Pa. $7.95

GUIDE TO OWL WATCHING IN NORTH AMERICA, Donald S. Heintzelman. Superb guide offers complete data and descriptions of 19 species: barn owl, screech owl, snowy owl, many more. Expert coverage of owl-watching equipment, conservation, migrations and invasions, etc. Guide to observing sites. 84 illustrations. xiii + 193pp. 5⅜ × 8½. 27344-X Pa. $7.95

MEDICINAL AND OTHER USES OF NORTH AMERICAN PLANTS: A Historical Survey with Special Reference to the Eastern Indian Tribes, Charlotte Erichsen-Brown. Chronological historical citations document 500 years of usage of plants, trees, shrubs native to eastern Canada, northeastern U.S. Also complete identifying information. 343 illustrations. 544pp. 6½ × 9¼. 25951-X Pa. $12.95

STORYBOOK MAZES, Dave Phillips. 23 stories and mazes on two-page spreads: Wizard of Oz, Treasure Island, Robin Hood, etc. Solutions. 64pp. 8¼ × 11.
23628-5 Pa. $2.95

NEGRO FOLK MUSIC, U.S.A., Harold Courlander. Noted folklorist's scholarly yet readable analysis of rich and varied musical tradition. Includes authentic versions of over 40 folk songs. Valuable bibliography and discography. xi + 324pp. 5⅜ × 8½. 27350-4 Pa. $7.95

MOVIE-STAR PORTRAITS OF THE FORTIES, John Kobal (ed.). 163 glamor, studio photos of 106 stars of the 1940s: Rita Hayworth, Ava Gardner, Marlon Brando, Clark Gable, many more. 176pp. 8⅜ × 11¼. 23546-7 Pa. $10.95

BENCHLEY LOST AND FOUND, Robert Benchley. Finest humor from early 30s, about pet peeves, child psychologists, post office and others. Mostly unavailable elsewhere. 73 illustrations by Peter Arno and others. 183pp. 5⅜ × 8½.
22410-4 Pa. $5.95

YEKL and THE IMPORTED BRIDEGROOM AND OTHER STORIES OF YIDDISH NEW YORK, Abraham Cahan. Film Hester Street based on Yekl (1896). Novel, other stories among first about Jewish immigrants on N.Y.'s East Side. 240pp. 5⅜ × 8½. 22427-9 Pa. $5.95

SELECTED POEMS, Walt Whitman. Generous sampling from *Leaves of Grass*. Twenty-four poems include "I Hear America Singing," "Song of the Open Road," "I Sing the Body Electric," "When Lilacs Last in the Dooryard Bloom'd," "O Captain! My Captain!"—all reprinted from an authoritative edition. Lists of titles and first lines. 128pp. 5³⁄₁₆ × 8¼. 26878-0 Pa. $1.00

THE BEST TALES OF HOFFMANN, E. T. A. Hoffmann. 10 of Hoffmann's most important stories: "Nutcracker and the King of Mice," "The Golden Flowerpot," etc. 458pp. 5⅜ × 8½. 21793-0 Pa. $8.95

FROM FETISH TO GOD IN ANCIENT EGYPT, E. A. Wallis Budge. Rich detailed survey of Egyptian conception of "God" and gods, magic, cult of animals, Osiris, more. Also, superb English translations of hymns and legends. 240 illustrations. 545pp. 5⅜ × 8½. 25803-3 Pa. $11.95

FRENCH STORIES/CONTES FRANÇAIS: A Dual-Language Book, Wallace Fowlie. Ten stories by French masters, Voltaire to Camus: "Micromegas" by Voltaire; "The Atheist's Mass" by Balzac; "Minuet" by de Maupassant; "The Guest" by Camus, six more. Excellent English translations on facing pages. Also French-English vocabulary list, exercises, more. 352pp. 5⅜ × 8½. 26443-2 Pa. $8.95

CHICAGO AT THE TURN OF THE CENTURY IN PHOTOGRAPHS: 122 Historic Views from the Collections of the Chicago Historical Society, Larry A. Viskochil. Rare large-format prints offer detailed views of City Hall, State Street, the Loop, Hull House, Union Station, many other landmarks, circa 1904–1913. Introduction. Captions. Maps. 144pp. 9⅜ × 12¼. 24656-6 Pa. $12.95

OLD BROOKLYN IN EARLY PHOTOGRAPHS, 1865–1929, William Lee Younger. Luna Park, Gravesend race track, construction of Grand Army Plaza, moving of Hotel Brighton, etc. 157 previously unpublished photographs. 165pp. 8⅞ × 11¾. 23587-4 Pa. $12.95

THE MYTHS OF THE NORTH AMERICAN INDIANS, Lewis Spence. Rich anthology of the myths and legends of the Algonquins, Iroquois, Pawnees and Sioux, prefaced by an extensive historical and ethnological commentary. 36 illustrations. 480pp. 5⅜ × 8½. 25967-6 Pa. $8.95

AN ENCYCLOPEDIA OF BATTLES: Accounts of Over 1,560 Battles from 1479 B.C. to the Present, David Eggenberger. Essential details of every major battle in recorded history from the first battle of Megiddo in 1479 B.C. to Grenada in 1984. List of Battle Maps. New Appendix covering the years 1967–1984. Index. 99 illustrations. 544pp. 6½ × 9¼. 24913-1 Pa. $14.95

SAILING ALONE AROUND THE WORLD, Captain Joshua Slocum. First man to sail around the world, alone, in small boat. One of great feats of seamanship told in delightful manner. 67 illustrations. 294pp. 5⅜ × 8½. 20326-3 Pa. $5.95

ANARCHISM AND OTHER ESSAYS, Emma Goldman. Powerful, penetrating, prophetic essays on direct action, role of minorities, prison reform, puritan hypocrisy, violence, etc. 271pp. 5⅜ × 8½. 22484-8 Pa. $5.95

MYTHS OF THE HINDUS AND BUDDHISTS, Ananda K. Coomaraswamy and Sister Nivedita. Great stories of the epics; deeds of Krishna, Shiva, taken from puranas, Vedas, folk tales; etc. 32 illustrations. 400pp. 5⅜ × 8½. 21759-0 Pa. $9.95

BEYOND PSYCHOLOGY, Otto Rank. Fear of death, desire of immortality, nature of sexuality, social organization, creativity, according to Rankian system. 291pp. 5⅜ × 8½. 20485-5 Pa. $7.95

A THEOLOGICO-POLITICAL TREATISE, Benedict Spinoza. Also contains unfinished Political Treatise. Great classic on religious liberty, theory of government on common consent. R. Elwes translation. Total of 421pp. 5⅜ × 8½. 20249-6 Pa. $7.95

MY BONDAGE AND MY FREEDOM, Frederick Douglass. Born a slave, Douglass became outspoken force in antislavery movement. The best of Douglass' autobiographies. Graphic description of slave life. 464pp. 5⅜ × 8½.   22457-0 Pa. $8.95

FOLLOWING THE EQUATOR: A Journey Around the World, Mark Twain. Fascinating humorous account of 1897 voyage to Hawaii, Australia, India, New Zealand, etc. Ironic, bemused reports on peoples, customs, climate, flora and fauna, politics, much more. 197 illustrations. 720pp. 5⅜ × 8½.   26113-1 Pa. $15.95

THE PEOPLE CALLED SHAKERS, Edward D. Andrews. Definitive study of Shakers: origins, beliefs, practices, dances, social organization, furniture and crafts, etc. 33 illustrations. 351pp. 5⅜ × 8½.   21081-2 Pa. $7.95

THE MYTHS OF GREECE AND ROME, H. A. Guerber. A classic of mythology, generously illustrated, long prized for its simple, graphic, accurate retelling of the principal myths of Greece and Rome, and for its commentary on their origins and significance. With 64 illustrations by Michelangelo, Raphael, Titian, Rubens, Canova, Bernini and others. 480pp. 5⅜ × 8½.   27584-1 Pa. $9.95

PSYCHOLOGY OF MUSIC, Carl E. Seashore. Classic work discusses music as a medium from psychological viewpoint. Clear treatment of physical acoustics, auditory apparatus, sound perception, development of musical skills, nature of musical feeling, host of other topics. 88 figures. 408pp. 5⅜ × 8½. 21851-1 Pa. $9.95

THE PHILOSOPHY OF HISTORY, Georg W. Hegel. Great classic of Western thought develops concept that history is not chance but rational process, the evolution of freedom. 457pp. 5⅜ × 8½.   20112-0 Pa. $8.95

THE BOOK OF TEA, Kakuzo Okakura. Minor classic of the Orient: entertaining, charming explanation, interpretation of traditional Japanese culture in terms of tea ceremony. 94pp. 5⅜ × 8½.   20070-1 Pa. $2.95

LIFE IN ANCIENT EGYPT, Adolf Erman. Fullest, most thorough, detailed older account with much not in more recent books, domestic life, religion, magic, medicine, commerce, much more. Many illustrations reproduce tomb paintings, carvings, hieroglyphs, etc. 597pp. 5⅜ × 8½.   22632-8 Pa. $9.95

SUNDIALS, Their Theory and Construction, Albert Waugh. Far and away the best, most thorough coverage of ideas, mathematics concerned, types, construction, adjusting anywhere. Simple, nontechnical treatment allows even children to build several of these dials. Over 100 illustrations. 230pp. 5⅜ × 8½.   22947-5 Pa. $5.95

DYNAMICS OF FLUIDS IN POROUS MEDIA, Jacob Bear. For advanced students of ground water hydrology, soil mechanics and physics, drainage and irrigation engineering, and more. 335 illustrations. Exercises, with answers. 784pp. 6⅛ × 9¼.   65675-6 Pa. $19.95

SONGS OF EXPERIENCE: Facsimile Reproduction with 26 Plates in Full Color, William Blake. 26 full-color plates from a rare 1826 edition. Includes "The Tyger," "London," "Holy Thursday," and other poems. Printed text of poems. 48pp. 5¼ × 7.
24636-1 Pa. $3.95

OLD-TIME VIGNETTES IN FULL COLOR, Carol Belanger Grafton (ed.). Over 390 charming, often sentimental illustrations, selected from archives of Victorian graphics—pretty women posing, children playing, food, flowers, kittens and puppies, smiling cherubs, birds and butterflies, much more. All copyright-free. 48pp. 9¼ × 12¼.   27269-9 Pa. $5.95

PERSPECTIVE FOR ARTISTS, Rex Vicat Cole. Depth, perspective of sky and sea, shadows, much more, not usually covered. 391 diagrams, 81 reproductions of drawings and paintings. 279pp. 5⅜ × 8½. 22487-2 Pa. $6.95

DRAWING THE LIVING FIGURE, Joseph Sheppard. Innovative approach to artistic anatomy focuses on specifics of surface anatomy, rather than muscles and bones. Over 170 drawings of live models in front, back and side views, and in widely varying poses. Accompanying diagrams. 177 illustrations. Introduction. Index. 144pp. 8⅜ × 11¼. 26723-7 Pa. $7.95

GOTHIC AND OLD ENGLISH ALPHABETS: 100 Complete Fonts, Dan X. Solo. Add power, elegance to posters, signs, other graphics with 100 stunning copyright-free alphabets: Blackstone, Dolbey, Germania, 97 more—including many lower-case, numerals, punctuation marks. 104pp. 8⅛ × 11. 24695-7 Pa. $7.95

HOW TO DO BEADWORK, Mary White. Fundamental book on craft from simple projects to five-bead chains and woven works. 106 illustrations. 142pp. 5⅜ × 8. 20697-1 Pa. $4.95

THE BOOK OF WOOD CARVING, Charles Marshall Sayers. Finest book for beginners discusses fundamentals and offers 34 designs. "Absolutely first rate . . . well thought out and well executed."—E. J. Tangerman. 118pp. 7¾ × 10⅝. 23654-4 Pa. $5.95

ILLUSTRATED CATALOG OF CIVIL WAR MILITARY GOODS: Union Army Weapons, Insignia, Uniform Accessories, and Other Equipment, Schuyler, Hartley, and Graham. Rare, profusely illustrated 1846 catalog includes Union Army uniform and dress regulations, arms and ammunition, coats, insignia, flags, swords, rifles, etc. 226 illustrations. 160pp. 9 × 12. 24939-5 Pa. $10.95

WOMEN'S FASHIONS OF THE EARLY 1900s: An Unabridged Republication of "New York Fashions, 1909," National Cloak & Suit Co. Rare catalog of mail-order fashions documents women's and children's clothing styles shortly after the turn of the century. Captions offer full descriptions, prices. Invaluable resource for fashion, costume historians. Approximately 725 illustrations. 128pp. 8⅜ × 11¼. 27276-1 Pa. $10.95

THE 1912 AND 1915 GUSTAV STICKLEY FURNITURE CATALOGS, Gustav Stickley. With over 200 detailed illustrations and descriptions, these two catalogs are essential reading and reference materials and identification guides for Stickley furniture. Captions cite materials, dimensions and prices. 112pp. 6½ × 9¼. 26676-1 Pa. $9.95

EARLY AMERICAN LOCOMOTIVES, John H. White, Jr. Finest locomotive engravings from early 19th century: historical (1804–74), main-line (after 1870), special, foreign, etc. 147 plates. 142pp. 11⅜ × 8¼. 22772-3 Pa. $8.95

THE TALL SHIPS OF TODAY IN PHOTOGRAPHS, Frank O. Braynard. Lavishly illustrated tribute to nearly 100 majestic contemporary sailing vessels: Amerigo Vespucci, Clearwater, Constitution, Eagle, Mayflower, Sea Cloud, Victory, many more. Authoritative captions provide statistics, background on each ship. 190 black-and-white photographs and illustrations. Introduction. 128pp. 8⅞ × 11¾. 27163-3 Pa. $12.95

EARLY NINETEENTH-CENTURY CRAFTS AND TRADES, Peter Stockham (ed.). Extremely rare 1807 volume describes to youngsters the crafts and trades of the day: brickmaker, weaver, dressmaker, bookbinder, ropemaker, saddler, many more. Quaint prose, charming illustrations for each craft. 20 black-and-white line illustrations. 192pp. 4⅜ × 6. 27293-1 Pa. $4.95

VICTORIAN FASHIONS AND COSTUMES FROM HARPER'S BAZAR, 1867–1898, Stella Blum (ed.). Day costumes, evening wear, sports clothes, shoes, hats, other accessories in over 1,000 detailed engravings. 320pp. 9⅜ × 12¼. 22990-4 Pa. $13.95

GUSTAV STICKLEY, THE CRAFTSMAN, Mary Ann Smith. Superb study surveys broad scope of Stickley's achievement, especially in architecture. Design philosophy, rise and fall of the Craftsman empire, descriptions and floor plans for many Craftsman houses, more. 86 black-and-white halftones. 31 line illustrations. Introduction. 208pp. 6½ × 9¼. 27210-9 Pa. $9.95

THE LONG ISLAND RAIL ROAD IN EARLY PHOTOGRAPHS, Ron Ziel. Over 220 rare photos, informative text document origin (1844) and development of rail service on Long Island. Vintage views of early trains, locomotives, stations, passengers, crews, much more. Captions. 8⅞ × 11¾. 26301-0 Pa. $13.95

THE BOOK OF OLD SHIPS: From Egyptian Galleys to Clipper Ships, Henry B. Culver. Superb, authoritative history of sailing vessels, with 80 magnificent line illustrations. Galley, bark, caravel, longship, whaler, many more. Detailed, informative text on each vessel by noted naval historian. Introduction. 256pp. 5⅜ × 8½. 27332-6 Pa. $6.95

TEN BOOKS ON ARCHITECTURE, Vitruvius. The most important book ever written on architecture. Early Roman aesthetics, technology, classical orders, site selection, all other aspects. Morgan translation. 331pp. 5⅜ × 8½. 20645-9 Pa. $8.95

THE HUMAN FIGURE IN MOTION, Eadweard Muybridge. More than 4,500 stopped-action photos, in action series, showing undraped men, women, children jumping, lying down, throwing, sitting, wrestling, carrying, etc. 390pp. 7⅞ × 10⅝. 20204-6 Clothbd. $24.95

TREES OF THE EASTERN AND CENTRAL UNITED STATES AND CANADA, William M. Harlow. Best one-volume guide to 140 trees. Full descriptions, woodlore, range, etc. Over 600 illustrations. Handy size. 288pp. 4½ × 6⅜. 20395-6 Pa. $5.95

SONGS OF WESTERN BIRDS, Dr. Donald J. Borror. Complete song and call repertoire of 60 western species, including flycatchers, juncoes, cactus wrens, many more—includes fully illustrated booklet. Cassette and manual 99913-0 $8.95

GROWING AND USING HERBS AND SPICES, Milo Miloradovich. Versatile handbook provides all the information needed for cultivation and use of all the herbs and spices available in North America. 4 illustrations. Index. Glossary. 236pp. 5⅜ × 8½. 25058-X Pa. $5.95

BIG BOOK OF MAZES AND LABYRINTHS, Walter Shepherd. 50 mazes and labyrinths in aH—classical, solid, ripple, and more—in one great volume. Perfect inexpensive puzzler for clever youngsters. Full solutions. 112pp. 8⅛ × 11. 22951-3 Pa. $3.95

PIANO TUNING, J. Cree Fischer. Clearest, best book for beginner, amateur. Simple repairs, raising dropped notes, tuning by easy method of flattened fifths. No previous skills needed. 4 illustrations. 201pp. 5⅜ × 8½. 23267-0 Pa. $5.95

A SOURCE BOOK IN THEATRICAL HISTORY, A. M. Nagler. Contemporary observers on acting, directing, make-up, costuming, stage props, machinery, scene design, from Ancient Greece to Chekhov. 611pp. 5⅜ × 8½. 20515-0 Pa. $11.95

THE COMPLETE NONSENSE OF EDWARD LEAR, Edward Lear. All nonsense limericks, zany alphabets, Owl and Pussycat, songs, nonsense botany, etc., illustrated by Lear. Total of 320pp. 5⅜ × 8½. (USO) 20167-8 Pa. $5.95

VICTORIAN PARLOUR POETRY: An Annotated Anthology, Michael R. Turner. 117 gems by Longfellow, Tennyson, Browning, many lesser-known poets. "The Village Blacksmith," "Curfew Must Not Ring Tonight," "Only a Baby Small," dozens more, often difficult to find elsewhere. Index of poets, titles, first lines. xxiii + 325pp. 5⅜ × 8¼. 27044-0 Pa. $8.95

DUBLINERS, James Joyce. Fifteen stories offer vivid, tightly focused observations of the lives of Dublin's poorer classes. At least one, "The Dead," is considered a masterpiece. Reprinted complete and unabridged from standard edition. 160pp. 5³⁄₁₆ × 8¼. 26870-5 Pa. $1.00

THE HAUNTED MONASTERY and THE CHINESE MAZE MURDERS, Robert van Gulik. Two full novels by van Gulik, set in 7th-century China, continue adventures of Judge Dee and his companions. An evil Taoist monastery, seemingly supernatural events; overgrown topiary maze hides strange crimes. 27 illustrations. 328pp. 5⅜ × 8½. 23502-5 Pa. $7.95

THE BOOK OF THE SACRED MAGIC OF ABRAMELIN THE MAGE, translated by S. MacGregor Mathers. Medieval manuscript of ceremonial magic. Basic document in Aleister Crowley, Golden Dawn groups. 268pp. 5⅜ × 8½. 23211-5 Pa. $7.95

NEW RUSSIAN-ENGLISH AND ENGLISH-RUSSIAN DICTIONARY, M. A. O'Brien. This is a remarkably handy Russian dictionary, containing a surprising amount of information, including over 70,000 entries. 366pp. 4½ × 6⅛. 20208-9 Pa. $8.95

HISTORIC HOMES OF THE AMERICAN PRESIDENTS, Second, Revised Edition, Irvin Haas. A traveler's guide to American Presidential homes, most open to the public, depicting and describing homes occupied by every American President from George Washington to George Bush. With visiting hours, admission charges, travel routes. 175 photographs. Index. 160pp. 8¼ × 11. 26751-2 Pa. $10.95

NEW YORK IN THE FORTIES, Andreas Feininger. 162 brilliant photographs by the well-known photographer, formerly with *Life* magazine. Commuters, shoppers, Times Square at night, much else from city at its peak. Captions by John von Hartz. 181pp. 9¼ × 10¾. 23585-8 Pa. $12.95

INDIAN SIGN LANGUAGE, William Tomkins. Over 525 signs developed by Sioux and other tribes. Written instructions and diagrams. Also 290 pictographs. 111pp. 6⅛ × 9¼. 22029-X Pa. $3.50

ANATOMY: A Complete Guide for Artists, Joseph Sheppard. A master of figure drawing shows artists how to render human anatomy convincingly. Over 460 illustrations. 224pp. 8⅜ × 11¼. 27279-6 Pa. $9.95

MEDIEVAL CALLIGRAPHY: Its History and Technique, Marc Drogin. Spirited history, comprehensive instruction manual covers 13 styles (ca. 4th century thru 15th). Excellent photographs; directions for duplicating medieval techniques with modern tools. 224pp. 8⅜ × 11¼. 26142-5 Pa. $11.95

DRIED FLOWERS: How to Prepare Them, Sarah Whitlock and Martha Rankin. Complete instructions on how to use silica gel, meal and borax, perlite aggregate, sand and borax, glycerine and water to create attractive permanent flower arrangements. 12 illustrations. 32pp. 5⅜ × 8½. 21802-3 Pa. $1.00

EASY-TO-MAKE BIRD FEEDERS FOR WOODWORKERS, Scott D. Campbell. Detailed, simple-to-use guide for designing, constructing, caring for and using feeders. Text, illustrations for 12 classic and contemporary designs. 96pp. 5⅜ × 8½. 25847-5 Pa. $2.95

OLD-TIME CRAFTS AND TRADES, Peter Stockham. An 1807 book created to teach children about crafts and trades open to them as future careers. It describes in detailed, nontechnical terms 24 different occupations, among them coachmaker, gardener, hairdresser, lacemaker, shoemaker, wheelwright, copper-plate printer, milliner, trunkmaker, merchant and brewer. Finely detailed engravings illustrate each occupation. 192pp. 4⅝ × 6. 27398-9 Pa. $4.95

THE HISTORY OF UNDERCLOTHES, C. Willett Cunnington and Phyllis Cunnington. Fascinating, well-documented survey covering six centuries of English undergarments, enhanced with over 100 illustrations: 12th-century laced-up bodice, footed long drawers (1795), 19th-century bustles, 19th-century corsets for men, Victorian "bust improvers," much more. 272pp. 5⅜ × 8¼. 27124-2 Pa. $9.95

ARTS AND CRAFTS FURNITURE: The Complete Brooks Catalog of 1912, Brooks Manufacturing Co. Photos and detailed descriptions of more than 150 now very collectible furniture designs from the Arts and Crafts movement depict davenports, settees, buffets, desks, tables, chairs, bedsteads, dressers and more, all built of solid, quarter-sawed oak. Invaluable for students and enthusiasts of antiques, Americana and the decorative arts. 80pp. 6½ × 9¼. 27471-3 Pa. $7.95

HOW WE INVENTED THE AIRPLANE: An Illustrated History, Orville Wright. Fascinating firsthand account covers early experiments, construction of planes and motors, first flights, much more. Introduction and commentary by Fred C. Kelly. 76 photographs. 96pp. 8¼ × 11. 25662-6 Pa. $7.95

THE ARTS OF THE SAILOR: Knotting, Splicing and Ropework, Hervey Garrett Smith. Indispensable shipboard reference covers tools, basic knots and useful hitches; handsewing and canvas work, more. Over 100 illustrations. Delightful reading for sea lovers. 256pp. 5⅜ × 8½. 26440-8 Pa. $7.95

FRANK LLOYD WRIGHT'S FALLINGWATER: The House and Its History, Second, Revised Edition, Donald Hoffmann. A total revision—both in text and illustrations—of the standard document on Fallingwater, the boldest, most personal architectural statement of Wright's mature years, updated with valuable new material from the recently opened Frank Lloyd Wright Archives. "Fascinating"—*The New York Times*. 116 illustrations. 128pp. 9¼ × 10¾. 27430-6 Pa. $10.95

PHOTOGRAPHIC SKETCHBOOK OF THE CIVIL WAR, Alexander Gardner. 100 photos taken on field during the Civil War. Famous shots of Manassas, Harper's Ferry, Lincoln, Richmond, slave pens, etc. 244pp. 10⅝ × 8¼.
22731-6 Pa. $9.95

FIVE ACRES AND INDEPENDENCE, Maurice G. Kains. Great back-to-the-land classic explains basics of self-sufficient farming. The one book to get. 95 illustrations. 397pp. 5⅜ × 8½. 20974-1 Pa. $6.95

SONGS OF EASTERN BIRDS, Dr. Donald J. Borror. Songs and calls of 60 species most common to eastern U.S.: warblers, woodpeckers, flycatchers, thrushes, larks, many more in high-quality recording. Cassette and manual 99912-2 $8.95

A MODERN HERBAL, Margaret Grieve. Much the fullest, most exact, most useful compilation of herbal material. Gigantic alphabetical encyclopedia, from aconite to zedoary, gives botanical information, medical properties, folklore, economic uses, much else. Indispensable to serious reader. 161 illustrations. 888pp. 6½ × 9¼. 2-vol. set. (USO) Vol. I: 22798-7 Pa. $9.95
Vol. II: 22799-5 Pa. $9.95

HIDDEN TREASURE MAZE BOOK, Dave Phillips. Solve 34 challenging mazes accompanied by heroic tales of adventure. Evil dragons, people-eating plants, bloodthirsty giants, many more dangerous adversaries lurk at every twist and turn. 34 mazes, stories, solutions. 48pp. 8¼ × 11. 24566-7 Pa. $2.95

LETTERS OF W. A. MOZART, Wolfgang A. Mozart. Remarkable letters show bawdy wit, humor, imagination, musical insights, contemporary musical world; includes some letters from Leopold Mozart. 276pp. 5⅜ × 8½. 22859-2 Pa. $6.95

BASIC PRINCIPLES OF CLASSICAL BALLET, Agrippina Vaganova. Great Russian theoretician, teacher explains methods for teaching classical ballet. 118 illustrations. 175pp. 5⅜ × 8½. 22036-2 Pa. $4.95

THE JUMPING FROG, Mark Twain. Revenge edition. The original story of The Celebrated Jumping Frog of Calaveras County, a hapless French translation, and Twain's hilarious "retranslation" from the French. 12 illustrations. 66pp. 5⅜ × 8½. 22686-7 Pa. $3.50

BEST REMEMBERED POEMS, Martin Gardner (ed.). The 126 poems in this superb collection of 19th- and 20th-century British and American verse range from Shelley's "To a Skylark" to the impassioned "Renascence" of Edna St. Vincent Millay and to Edward Lear's whimsical "The Owl and the Pussycat." 224pp. 5⅜ × 8½. 27165-X Pa. $4.95

COMPLETE SONNETS, William Shakespeare. Over 150 exquisite poems deal with love, friendship, the tyranny of time, beauty's evanescence, death and other themes in language of remarkable power, precision and beauty. Glossary of archaic terms. 80pp. 5³⁄₁₆ × 8¼. 26686-9 Pa. $1.00

BODIES IN A BOOKSHOP, R. T. Campbell. Challenging mystery of blackmail and murder with ingenious plot and superbly drawn characters. In the best tradition of British suspense fiction. 192pp. 5⅜ × 8½. 24720-1 Pa. $5.95

THE WIT AND HUMOR OF OSCAR WILDE, Alvin Redman (ed.). More than 1,000 ripostes, paradoxes, wisecracks: Work is the curse of the drinking classes; I can resist everything except temptation; etc. 258pp. 5⅜ × 8½. 20602-5 Pa. $4.95

SHAKESPEARE LEXICON AND QUOTATION DICTIONARY, Alexander Schmidt. Full definitions, locations, shades of meaning in every word in plays and poems. More than 50,000 exact quotations. 1,485pp. 6½ × 9¼. 2-vol. set.
Vol. 1: 22726-X Pa. $15.95
Vol. 2: 22727-8 Pa. $15.95

SELECTED POEMS, Emily Dickinson. Over 100 best-known, best-loved poems by one of America's foremost poets, reprinted from authoritative early editions. No comparable edition at this price. Index of first lines. 64pp. 5$\frac{3}{16}$ × 8¼.
26466-1 Pa. $1.00

CELEBRATED CASES OF JUDGE DEE (DEE GOONG AN), translated by Robert van Gulik. Authentic 18th-century Chinese detective novel; Dee and associates solve three interlocked cases. Led to van Gulik's own stories with same characters. Extensive introduction. 9 illustrations. 237pp. 5⅜ × 8½.
23337-5 Pa. $5.95

THE MALLEUS MALEFICARUM OF KRAMER AND SPRENGER, translated by Montague Summers. Full text of most important witchhunter's "bible," used by both Catholics and Protestants. 278pp. 6⅝ × 10. 22802-9 Pa. $10.95

SPANISH STORIES/CUENTOS ESPAÑOLES: A Dual-Language Book, Angel Flores (ed.). Unique format offers 13 great stories in Spanish by Cervantes, Borges, others. Faithful English translations on facing pages. 352pp. 5⅜ × 8½.
25399-6 Pa. $8.95

THE CHICAGO WORLD'S FAIR OF 1893: A Photographic Record, Stanley Appelbaum (ed.). 128 rare photos show 200 buildings, Beaux-Arts architecture, Midway, original Ferris Wheel, Edison's kinetoscope, more. Architectural emphasis; full text. 116pp. 8¼ × 11. 23990-X Pa. $9.95

OLD QUEENS, N.Y., IN EARLY PHOTOGRAPHS, Vincent F. Seyfried and William Asadorian. Over 160 rare photographs of Maspeth, Jamaica, Jackson Heights, and other areas. Vintage views of DeWitt Clinton mansion, 1939 World's Fair and more. Captions. 192pp. 8⅞ × 11. 26358-4 Pa. $12.95

CAPTURED BY THE INDIANS: 15 Firsthand Accounts, 1750–1870, Frederick Drimmer. Astounding true historical accounts of grisly torture, bloody conflicts, relentless pursuits, miraculous escapes and more, by people who lived to tell the tale. 384pp. 5⅜ × 8½. 24901-8 Pa. $7.95

THE WORLD'S GREAT SPEECHES, Lewis Copeland and Lawrence W. Lamm (eds.). Vast collection of 278 speeches of Greeks to 1970. Powerful and effective models; unique look at history. 842pp. 5⅜ × 8½. 20468-5 Pa. $13.95

THE BOOK OF THE SWORD, Sir Richard F. Burton. Great Victorian scholar/adventurer's eloquent, erudite history of the "queen of weapons"—from prehistory to early Roman Empire. Evolution and development of early swords, variations (sabre, broadsword, cutlass, scimitar, etc.), much more. 336pp. 6⅛ × 9¼. 25434-8 Pa. $8.95

AUTOBIOGRAPHY: The Story of My Experiments with Truth, Mohandas K. Gandhi. Boyhood, legal studies, purification, the growth of the Satyagraha (nonviolent protest) movement. Critical, inspiring work of the man responsible for the freedom of India. 480pp. 5⅜ × 8½. (USO)   24593-4 Pa. $7.95

CELTIC MYTHS AND LEGENDS, T. W. Rolleston. Masterful retelling of Irish and Welsh stories and tales. Cuchulain, King Arthur, Deirdre, the Grail, many more. First paperback edition. 58 full-page illustrations. 512pp. 5⅜ × 8½.
26507-2 Pa. $9.95

THE PRINCIPLES OF PSYCHOLOGY, William James. Famous long course complete, unabridged. Stream of thought, time perception, memory, experimental methods; great work decades ahead of its time. 94 figures. 1,391pp. 5⅜ × 8½. 2-vol. set.
Vol. I: 20381-6 Pa. $12.95
Vol. II: 20382-4 Pa. $12.95

THE WORLD AS WILL AND REPRESENTATION, Arthur Schopenhauer. Definitive English translation of Schopenhauer's life work, correcting more than 1,000 errors, omissions in earlier translations. Translated by E. F. J. Payne. Total of 1,269pp. 5⅜ × 8½. 2-vol. set.
Vol. 1: 21761-2 Pa. $10.95
Vol. 2: 21762-0 Pa. $11.95

MAGIC AND MYSTERY IN TIBET, Madame Alexandra David-Neel. Experiences among lamas, magicians, sages, sorcerers, Bonpa wizards. A true psychic discovery. 32 illustrations. 321pp. 5⅜ × 8½. (USO)   22682-4 Pa. $8.95

THE EGYPTIAN BOOK OF THE DEAD, E. A. Wallis Budge. Complete reproduction of Ani's papyrus, finest ever found. Full hieroglyphic text, interlinear transliteration, word-for-word translation, smooth translation. 533pp. 6½ × 9¼.
21866-X Pa. $9.95

MATHEMATICS FOR THE NONMATHEMATICIAN, Morris Kline. Detailed, college-level treatment of mathematics in cultural and historical context, with numerous exercises. Recommended Reading Lists. Tables. Numerous figures. 641pp. 5⅜ × 8½.   24823-2 Pa. $11.95

THEORY OF WING SECTIONS: Including a Summary of Airfoil Data, Ira H. Abbott and A. E. von Doenhoff. Concise compilation of subsonic aerodynamic characteristics of NACA wing sections, plus description of theory. 350pp. of tables. 693pp. 5⅜ × 8½.   60586-8 Pa. $13.95

THE RIME OF THE ANCIENT MARINER, Gustave Doré, S. T. Coleridge. Doré's finest work; 34 plates capture moods, subtleties of poem. Flawless full-size reproductions printed on facing pages with authoritative text of poem. "Beautiful. Simply beautiful."—*Publisher's Weekly.* 77pp. 9¼ × 12.   22305-1 Pa. $5.95

NORTH AMERICAN INDIAN DESIGNS FOR ARTISTS AND CRAFTS-PEOPLE, Eva Wilson. Over 360 authentic copyright-free designs adapted from Navajo blankets, Hopi pottery, Sioux buffalo hides, more. Geometrics, symbolic figures, plant and animal motifs, etc. 128pp. 8⅜ × 11. (EUK)   25341-4 Pa. $7.95

SCULPTURE: Principles and Practice, Louis Slobodkin. Step-by-step approach to clay, plaster, metals, stone; classical and modern. 253 drawings, photos. 255pp. 8⅛ × 11.   22960-2 Pa. $9.95

CATALOG OF DOVER BOOKS

THE INFLUENCE OF SEA POWER UPON HISTORY, 1660–1783, A. T. Mahan. Influential classic of naval history and tactics still used as text in war colleges. First paperback edition. 4 maps. 24 battle plans. 640pp. 5⅜ × 8½.
25509-3 Pa. $12.95

THE STORY OF THE TITANIC AS TOLD BY ITS SURVIVORS, Jack Winocour (ed.). What it was really like. Panic, despair, shocking inefficiency, and a little heroism. More thrilling than any fictional account. 26 illustrations. 320pp. 5⅜ × 8½.
20610-6 Pa. $7.95

FAIRY AND FOLK TALES OF THE IRISH PEASANTRY, William Butler Yeats (ed.). Treasury of 64 tales from the twilight world of Celtic myth and legend: "The Soul Cages," "The Kildare Pooka," "King O'Toole and his Goose," many more. Introduction and Notes by W. B. Yeats. 352pp. 5⅜ × 8½.
26941-8 Pa. $7.95

BUDDHIST MAHAYANA TEXTS, E. B. Cowell and Others (eds.). Superb, accurate translations of basic documents in Mahayana Buddhism, highly important in history of religions. The Buddha-karita of Asvaghosha, Larger Sukhavativyuha, more. 448pp. 5⅜ × 8½. ,
25552-2 Pa. $9.95

ONE TWO THREE . . . INFINITY: Facts and Speculations of Science, George Gamow. Great physicist's fascinating, readable overview of contemporary science: number theory, relativity, fourth dimension, entropy, genes, atomic structure, much more. 128 illustrations. Index. 352pp. 5⅜ × 8½.
25664-2 Pa. $8.95

ENGINEERING IN HISTORY, Richard Shelton Kirby, et al. Broad, nontechnical survey of history's major technological advances: birth of Greek science, industrial revolution, electricity and applied science, 20th-century automation, much more. 181 illustrations. ". . . excellent . . ."—Isis. Bibliography. vii + 530pp. 5⅜ × 8¼.
26412-2 Pa. $14.95